MOTIVATED MONEY

YOU'VE INVESTED WELL?
COMPARED TO WHAT?

Peter Thornhill

Peter Thornhill was educated in Melbourne, and has worked in the finance service industry for almost 40 years. Between 1971 and 1982, Peter worked as an investment adviser with a London merchant bank. He was appointed a director of a leading United Kingdom Unit Trust group in 1984. Returning to Australia, Peter worked for several investment groups, including a period as General Manager of MLC.

Peter is now the principal of his own business: Motivated Money. His extensive experience, insights into wealth creation and entertaining style make him one of Australia's most sought after presenters. He is also a financial commentator in print and electronic media.

*I would like to give special thanks
to Tom Reddacliff and Michael Toal.*

First published 2002
Revised 2003
This revised edition published 2005 by
Motivated Money
21A Baldwin Street
GORDON NSW 2072

Email: peter@motivatedmoney.com.au
www.motivatedmoney.com
Phone: 02 9498 5053
Fax: 02 9498 5233

Made and printed in Australia
Design and layout Garnish Design
Production and editorial by The Learning Team
Logo design by Me, Myself & I

CONTENTS

FOREWORD

This book has been a dream of mine for a number of years. In my work in the financial services industry, I make hundreds of presentations each year to people who are trying to make sense of their financial futures. It sounds dry and dull — explaining wise investment principles. But it involves more than that — much more: I am talking to people about their dreams — what they want from their lives; and sometimes I am discussing their nightmares.

I would love a dollar for every time I have had people say to me, 'Why didn't I know you 10 years ago?' Often they will add, 'Have you written this down anywhere?' Well, now I have.

I wrote this book with two purposes in mind. The first is this: I want to change people's perceptions about wealth creation. Psychologists have long told us: *Perception is reality*. Optimists look at the world in terms of opportunities and challenges; pessimists see the same world as being full of dangers and pitfalls.

We all have our own perceptions when it comes to money; we have a perception of our position in the financial *pecking order*. In this book I discuss how our perceptions are formed and how these affect the financial decisions we make. I like to call them *conditioned reflexes*.

The second purpose is to satisfy a growing demand for basic investment knowledge. Most of us know how to spend money, but very few of us know how to make it. The information and technology age has delivered more and more information; giving us the perception that we have more knowledge and can conquer areas outside our expertise. Sadly, this is not so. Knowledge allows us to utilise information, and that eventually empowers us. Information without knowledge is at best useless, and at worst it can be dangerous.

This is especially true in the area of personal finance. Computer trading systems release vast amounts of information that anyone can access. These systems offer people opportunities to invest; I call this *masquerade investing*. People who are attracted into such schemes are often involved in what amounts to computerised gambling.

Information isn't knowledge and knowledge isn't wisdom.

There are hundreds of books on *how* to make money. This is not a book about how to *get rich quick;* it doesn't offer a magic formula. Underlying this book is an important assumption: making money without having a dream to fulfil is pointless and obscene.

This book is for people who have a clear vision — a dream or goal — something they wish to achieve. When some people think about their financial future, they ask the question: How much do I need? How much is enough?

I believe these are the wrong questions. Is *enough money* all you need to make your life *comfortable* and *fulfilling?* Too often, the accumulation of wealth becomes the end in itself, the goal to be achieved. And when is enough, enough?

I hope it gives you a sense of the book's philosophy: to give you empowering information in a simple, straightforward manner.

As a child, I read a story called *Frederick*. It is a story that has stayed with me all my adult life. It's about a group of field mice that have their home in an old stone wall that runs along a meadow where cows and horses graze. The farmer abandoned the farm long ago so the barn and granary stand empty. Since winter is not far off the mice are busy gathering corn, nuts, wheat and straw. They work all day and night — all, except for Frederick.

The others ask Frederick, 'Why don't you work?'

'I do work, I'm gathering sun rays for the cold, dark, winter days.'

Later they ask him again, and he replies, 'I'm gathering colours, because in winter everything is grey.'

Winter is fast approaching, and the mice are still working hard, but Frederick appears to be half asleep.

'Are you dreaming Frederick?' they ask reproachfully. 'Oh no, I am gathering words, for the winter days are long and many, and we will run out of things to say.'

Winter arrives and the five little mice take to their hideout in the old stonewall.

In the beginning there is plenty to eat and stories to be told, but little by little their store disappears. It is cold, they are hungry and now no one feels like chatting.

'What about your supplies, Frederick?' they ask.

And Frederick begins to tell them about the golden rays of the sun, and the warmth of summer fields; about the warm brown earth, and how the sun and the water combined to bring forth blue periwinkles and red poppies and yellow wheat. The other mice close their eyes. And now they can see the blue sky and the green leaves of the berry bushes. They relive the summer that seemed so far away.

There is more to life than the accumulation of wealth. Our task is, in part, to develop a clear vision of what is important to us — the things we truly value. That is the dream that will sustain us, the thing that will guide our decisions and our actions.

Put simply, *your choice* in the short term (a season) will have the greatest impact on your long-term dreams and ambitions.

In recent times, I've become increasingly interested in the notion of Emotional Intelligence — or EQ. We used to think that intelligence was our most powerful attribute: that the higher the IQ, the smarter the person. The definition of intelligence quotient (IQ) is *'a number indicating a person's level of intelligence: it is the mental age (as shown by intelligence tests) multiplied by 100 and divided by the chronological age.'* Most of us know people with high IQs who are anything but smart.

In his book *Emotional Intelligence*, published in 1996, Daniel Goleman wrote about the nature of success. The possession of technical skills is increasingly valued in our information- and knowledge-based society — and it is one of the keys to success. He quotes a popular joke: *'What do you call a nerd fifteen years from now? The answer: Boss!'*

But even more important than technical skill is emotional intelligence; it is this that gives people the *'added edge'*. He goes on to argue: *'Much evidence testifies that people who are emotionally adept — who know and manage their own feelings well, and who read and deal effectively with other people's feelings — are at an advantage in any domain in life.'*

Such people cope more effectively not only in intimate relationships, but also in *'the unspoken rules that govern success in organisational politics'*, and they master *'the habits of mind that foster their own productivity.'*

Goleman's warning to those lacking in these characteristics is clear: *'...people who cannot marshall some control over their emotional life fight inner battles that sabotage their ability for focussed work and clear thought.'*

This book is aimed squarely at those people with emotional intelligence. After all, no book has the whole answer — life is not that simple.

I cannot make you rich. Only you can achieve that goal; it's up to you to decide how much is enough. But here is the key point: **Whether your primary goals in life are personal or altruistic, striving for intelligent goals gives meaning to life.**

Helen Keller wrote: *'Security is an illusion. Life is either a daring adventure or it is nothing.'*

CHAPTER ONE
WHAT IS YOUR BENCHMARK?

When it comes to investments, people are often naïve in the attitudes they take. I commonly hear people say, 'I've done well.' If I press them a little, they will say, 'My investments are worth a lot more now than when I first invested.' On the surface, this looks plausible. But the question that needs to be asked is: 'You've done well — compared to what? What benchmark are you measuring your success against?'

When investing, we tend to apply very subjective parameters in gauging our success. We compare different assets over different time frames, and too often ignore after-tax results, preferring instead the rosier but less honest pre-tax result. For most of us, the perception that we have done well is nothing more than that: a perception. We usually base the measurement on someone else lower down the ladder.

In this chapter, I want to explore this issue in detail. When it comes to investments, what does it mean to do *well?* We'll start with some of the basic concepts.

Most people have heard of the All Ordinaries Index — after all, it's mentioned in the news every day. However, very few have a clear grasp of what makes up this index. Despite this, many people follow it on a daily basis and it can often set the mood.

A plummeting index means depressed speculators; a rising index means happy speculators. It has always puzzled me why people become so involved with something they don't really understand. Even more puzzling is the fact that few people make any attempt to find out. No wonder there are nasty shocks from time to time.

The Australian Stock Exchange changed the All Ordinaries Index in April 2000. It now consists of 500 of the top Australian companies. Prior to April 2000 it consisted of approximately 225 companies. There are 1,604 companies listed on the exchange, and the largest 500 companies represent 96 per cent of the Australian share market (by market capitalisation). The remaining 1,104 companies represent 4 per cent of industry value (Source: ASX Website April 2003). Many of the companies that make up this 4 per cent are the *penny dreadfuls;* investors often *play* with these. They are often priced at 10 cents or less and you get a lot of them for your $1,000 punt.

THE THREE PRIMARY SHARE MARKET INDICES

The All Ordinaries, the Industrials Index and the Resources Index are the three primary index used to track the health of investments. The graph on the next page shows the performance of these three indices over a 25 year period. These are price indices alone. The dividends paid by these companies over the period have been ignored.

Price Indices
Value of $100,000 invested December 1979 - 2004

Source: Reuters

THE RESOURCES INDEX

The Resources Index shows the aggregate value of Australian resource companies. These are basically mining companies; they dig things out of the ground: coal, oil, diamonds, aluminum, gold, and so on.

THE INDUSTRIALS INDEX

The Industrials Index refers to manufacturing and/or service companies. They provide the goods and services that make our lives livable — food companies, banks, insurance, retailers, manufacturers and so on. Open the centre pages of the Australian Financial Review and you will see the industrial and resource companies listed each day under separate headings.

THE ALL ORDINARIES INDEX

At June 2003 the All Ordinaries Index consisted of approximately 85 per cent industrial companies and 15 per cent resource companies. This needs to be seen in the context of the rapid changes that have occurred in recent times. It was only about two decades ago that the All Ordinaries consisted of 70 per cent Resources and only 30 per cent Industrials. If today, 70 per cent of the wealth we enjoy as individuals and collectively as a nation was reliant on resources, we would be in a very sorry state indeed! It was the industrial and service companies that saved us during this period. Now they produce the bulk of the wealth we enjoy as a nation. We have become an industrialised nation rather than a resource dustbin. However, even that is changing; now we need to become a nation striving for technological and intellectual excellence. That is where our future lies.

What the table below demonstrates is the relative value of the different parts of the share market. The share market is not homogenous, even though some people have misconceptions to the contrary; different parts of it do different things at different times. In times of *irrational exuberance* some people rush at this thing called the *market,* intent on creating wealth overnight. They invest in a company and wait for it to double. Very often, they punt on what looks an exciting resource stock. Having taken the plunge, they expect high returns — the kind of performance that *industrial* stocks sometimes produce, but are surprised and disappointed when all they get is resources performance.

Rise in original investment — share prices alone
December 1979 to 2004

Resources	4.9 times
Industrials	13.2 times
All Ordinaries	8.1 times

Source: S&P ASX

People are free to invest wherever they choose, but it is essential to understand that the share market consists of many different components, and these components do not perform in a uniform manner. Understanding this should help you avoid surprises and perhaps some disappointment.

An investment in Resource companies 25 years ago would now be worth just over four times the original investment, in price terms alone. The All Ordinaries has returned just over eight times and Industrial companies have returned just over thirteen times the original investment.

This information provides the *benchmarks* by which to measure our progress. In the context of these benchmarks, we can now judge just how well we have done.

If we quadrupled our money over 25 years have we done well? If we have increased our money eight-fold, have we done well? If we now have thirteen times our original investment, or twenty times or thirty times our money, have we done well? For most people the answer is, they don't know.

Most people are happy enough if they have more than when they started. My personal investment benchmark is the Industrials Index.

THE POWER OF DIVIDENDS

If we now include dividends, we can get an idea of the total value that these businesses have offered shareholders over this time period. The next graph shows the ACCUMULATION Indices. The graph on page 3 showed the way in which the face value of the shares fared over the 25-year period. The graph that follows on page 6 shows what would have happened had the income or dividends each year been reinvested back into the companies. (This is the equivalent of taking up an offer to participate in a dividend reinvestment plan with a public company.)

As you can see, Resource companies with 25 years of dividends reinvested fared least well. Resource companies are notoriously poor dividend payers; they tend to spend much of what they make looking for more buried treasure. In addition to this, resources like gold and metal ores are commodities, and there is not a lot of value added by digging them out of the ground. The major part of the return comes from digging vast quantities.

The greatest value added for the human race comes from manufacturing, technological and intellectual expertise. These are elements that have improved our living standards.

Reinvest the dividends from investment in the All Ordinaries, and your return is more than doubled, rising to over 22 times the original investment. The Industrials, on the other hand, gives you over 43 times your money. Here we begin to see the power of the income stream that will be revealed more and more in later chapters.

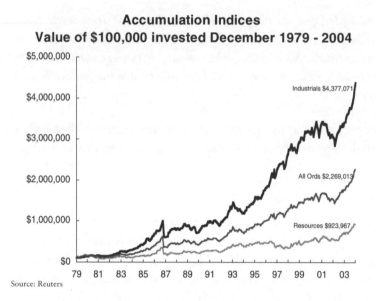

Accumulation Indices
Value of $100,000 invested December 1979 - 2004

Source: Reuters

Notice that dividends account for more than half the total value that industrial companies offer their shareholders. With dividends reinvested the value goes from just over 13 times to just over 43 times your original investment.

Rise in original investment — includes:
(a) the return on share prices alone, and
(b) share prices and dividends reinvested — accumulation

December 1979 to 2004

	(a) Share Price only	(b) Dividends Reinvested — Accumulation
Resources	4.9 times	9.2 times
Industrials	13.2 times	43.7 times
All Ordinaries	8.1 times	22.6 times

Source: S&P ASX

6

We need to go beyond seeing shares as purely growth assets. This *one-dimensional* view of assets remains the biggest trap for potential investors. This means that if we are just buying shares in order to then sell them in order to try and buy *better shares,* we could miss out on more than half the value that they have to offer. Frequently buying and selling, we may not hold the shares when they pay dividends. Share traders do not care about ex-dividend or dividend payment dates; they are there to benefit from a fluctuation in the price, which is defined as *speculation.*

It does not matter what we do in life — in our careers, business or personal relationships — it is important we do it well. Many of us feel that whatever we do will only impact on us. This is a very narrow view of life; most things we do on a daily basis have an impact on other peoples' lives. We are inextricably linked to the rest of humanity whether we like it or not! Choose an appropriate benchmark in one or more aspects of your life and prepare to be tested. The hallmark of people with no benchmarks or standards is mediocrity.

CHAPTER TWO
ARE YOU THE BIGGEST FOOL?

In the previous chapter we looked at two dimensions of an asset: its value and its capacity to generate income. In this chapter we will talk about the dangers of focusing on only one dimension of an asset. These examples should be very familiar to many.

Our focus on asset accumulation and asset price makes us aware of the total *monetary* value of our belongings. How many of us have mentally added up the *total value* of all our possessions and felt a warm inner glow as we realised just how wealthy we were becoming. This one-dimensional view of our possessions is a trap we have acquired for a number of historical reasons.

Anything that has a price we consider an asset. Unfortunately it is not true.

WHAT IS AN ASSET?

An asset is defined as something that pays you, something that brings us a return. A liability is defined as something you have to pay for. Thus we may add our car to the asset side of our balance sheet because it has a *value* (it cost me $50,000 — it's a valuable item). However, it costs us substantial amounts every year to run and maintain, and in most cases declines in value with time. This makes our car a liability.

THE INVESTMENT *FOOD* CHAIN

Since the human race began to walk upright on this planet we have had three primary assets available for investment. I describe this as the *Investment Food Chain*. At the top of the *Investment Food Chain* is the ultimate predator, productive enterprise, business or shares. In the middle of the *Investment Food Chain* is shelter or property. At the bottom of the *Investment Food Chain* is money lending. This primary food chain hasn't changed in thousands of years, and although we now have many variations, these remain the core three available to us.

There are many other things we call assets that fail the fundamental test: does it generate income?

The gold bar buried under the house — how much income does it generate? The vintage cars we collect — how much income do they generate? The antique furniture, jewellery, stamps, wine, artwork, etc. — how much income do they generate?

Each of these relies on a system that I call, 'The bigger fool than thou'. The only way we will derive value is to find a bigger fool than us who will pay more than we paid in the first place. They produce NO income. They can only produce a capital gain or loss. They are one-dimensional.

Before all the vintage car dealers, antique dealers and jewellers jump up and down, let me clarify this point. You are involved in a business; you buy items which you then sell for a profit. You are turning merchandise over and generating an income from constant trading in these items. Most of you have expertise in these areas. It is this expertise that gives dealing in these items value. If you have no expertise, then your life as an expert in any of these industries is likely to be short lived. Very different from the rest of us who tend to hold them longer term for their beauty or utility perhaps hoping for a profit from the sale at some time in the future.

Look around. Whilst I will not deny the *grin* factor associated with many of these things, consider some of your most prized possessions, particularly those that you hold for investment value as opposed to beauty or utility. Are you potentially the biggest fool? And remember — if you wish to own liabilities in retirement, make sure that you own the assets as well to generate the income you will need to pay for them.

INVESTING VERSUS SPECULATING

It is instructive to look at the definition of two other words at this time. Let's consider the definitions of *invest* and *speculate;* this will help to give us a better understanding of the point I am making.

Dictionaries make a clear distinction between the two terms. To INVEST is to put money into a business with the clear purpose of making a profit; when we invest, we expect that our investment will provide us with income or profit.

When we SPECULATE, we buy or sell commodities or stocks or land in the HOPE that there will be an unexpected rise in the price. To speculate is to take part in a risky venture. We are gambling, taking the chance that we'll be lucky, that we'll make huge profits. But there is no certainty, and much risk.

Most of us have a perception of what these words mean and there lies the danger. For example, if you acquired Telstra, Qantas, Commonwealth Bank or Woolworths shares in the original floats and sold them later for a *profit,* you could assume that you had *invested* in businesses. This was not the case. You merely speculated. The definition of invest has an implied timeframe associated with it.

People who run a business and who invest their money and time in that enterprise don't do it just so they can sell it at the end of the year to start the whole process over again.

Most businesses are run on the basis of producing an ongoing profit stream, year after year, for the owners, whether private or public. Commonwealth Bank shares that were bought and sold in the initial float were not investment — they were speculatory. The stock was not held long enough for people to enjoy any of the profits that the Commonwealth Bank is producing for shareholders over time.

Too often, speculation is described as investment simply because of our acceptance of sloppy language or the belief that the only way you make money is by buying and selling. Unfortunately, the press constantly reinforces this erroneous view. High profile individuals who speculate with their wealth are described as investors. This view often attracts new players into the game: 'So that's what investing is about — I'd better get on the bandwagon.'

In our working lives these issues seem to have less importance. In the financial arena we are focused on our careers and moving them forward in a meaningful way. For many of us this means buying *liabilities* that help us define ourselves in society. Houses, cars, boats... all these things help us to clarify for ourselves our *slot in the pecking order*. Some people become obsessive in their pursuit of these things, in this relentless pursuit of status, and in doing so ruin not only their own lives but also those of friends and family. This is where Emotional Intelligence becomes of paramount importance. Without sensible goals and a dream, wealth creation and its trappings become meaningless.

When we reach retirement, the assets we have worked so hard for must now start working for us. We have expended our hard earned income to acquire them; now they need to work for us. They need to generate enough income to sustain us for the rest of our lives. If however, we have spent our lives accumulating liabilities, then the future will look bleak. As much as we can enjoy the fact that our *liabilities* are worth money, as much as we can bask in other people's envy, if they generate no income then we have a problem.

If someone retires with $3 million we presume they have done well. If however, this consists of a $1 million house, a $1 million dollar boat and two $500,000 cars; how will their retirement shape up? Where is the money going to come from to maintain these liabilities? Don't think it will come from the Old Age Pension!

As much as they may enjoy the status ownership of these liabilities confers, without income they cannot afford them, and the realisation that their perceived status will diminish is not welcome. Many families will maintain a family home purely for emotional reasons, long after its *use by* date has passed. In many instances this can place a crippling burden on one generation in an attempt to pass on something of value to the next generation.

We can accumulate assets that will pay us in retirement and, if necessary, enable us to continue to hold liabilities that give us pleasure. The trick is to own the right assets — assets that generate income, that will grow in value over the long term and enable us to pursue the rest of our lives with as much passion and pleasure as we can muster.

CHAPTER THREE
TWO-DIMENSIONAL ASSETS

You may recall that in Chapter One – where I covered All Ordinaries, Industrials and Resources – we discussed benchmarks. Those benchmarks included two elements: price and dividends (income). In this chapter, I will expand further on those two elements.

1. THE VALUE OF THE ASSET

One indicator of the value of an asset is its purchase price — as in the case of shares and property. In the case of bank deposits, it is the amount deposited. What then happens to these values in the future is important.

2. THE INCOME STREAM IT GENERATES

An asset should generate an income stream. It is one of the aims of this book to try to impress upon you the important role that income plays in defining the long-term value of the assets you own.

For shares, it is the profits and dividends they pay; for property, the rent that we receive; and for bank deposits, it is the interest that is earned.

Future chapters explore these two elements (capital value and income-earning potential), and how they work together to give us the total return (the total value) of any asset. If you don't understand immediately, be patient. In the past, the financial services industry has made too much use of complex language and mind-numbing jargon. Part of my mission in this book is to challenge much of the financial education you may have received.

DANGEROUS MESSAGES ABOUT INCOME IN RETIREMENT

Capital value and income generating potential play the most significant role during the two main phases of our lives: the working years and retirement. Whilst working, we focus on wealth accumulation; often we judge our progress by the sum total of the *things* we own. Once we have retired, our focus shifts to income generation. We are taught to invest in *growth assets* during our working life, and then switch to *income assets* in retirement.

THIS IS WRONG AND HAS ALWAYS BEEN WRONG

All assets have the same underlying characteristics; just because we happen to focus on one at a particular time should not blind us to this fact. This short-term attitude has ruined many retirements. It has also created immense stress. A person retires and receives what seems a very large lump sum. However their whole future depends on how well they invest. They were never taught about managing money and what should be the beginning of the sweetest period of their lives can often turn stressful and sour.

The financial planning and fund management industries have tended to follow and maintain this artificial division of assets. We will often find the list of managed products in the daily financial press separated into *income funds* and *growth funds*. As a result we tend to end up with a one-dimensional view of most assets.

Some investments — term deposits, mortgage trusts, debentures and the like — are classified as income investments, primarily because of their high yields and stable asset base. Growth investments, on the other hand, provide low yields and have a fluctuating asset base. Shares tend to head the category of growth investments. Because of our different needs at different points in our lives, we are often told we must rearrange our assets as we move through life.

This is a common misconception that has existed for many decades. It is important to understand that **every** asset has two-dimensions: capital value and income. We ignore this fact at our peril. If we only focus on one aspect this gives us a very distorted view of the potential return from the asset. It means we run the risk of ignoring a significant part of the total return.

For most income assets, the comparison is straightforward: a 7 per cent yield is better than a 4 per cent yield; the 7 per cent yield will bring more money into our bank account. With growth assets, income doesn't even enter into the equation. For example, here are some typical questions asked about shares, property or other growth *assets:* Is the price high? Is the price low? Will the price go up or down?

These issues give shares, in particular, their speculative nature in most people's minds. Buyers can often be paralysed by short-term decisions they find impossible to make.

For example: *If I wait, the price might fall, in which case I can buy cheaper. On the flipside, if I buy now the price might fall and I'll lose money!*

This obsession with price totally ignores the second part of the return from shares: dividends (or income). I will talk about the importance of income and investment time frames throughout this book.

WE MUST INCREASE OUR INVESTMENT TIME FRAME!

Investing is a bit like the weather: one day fine and the next day stormy. Short term or speculative investment decisions are about as reliable as forecasting the weather day by day. Meteorologists are notoriously poor at forecasting tomorrow's weather conditions and are subject to considerable cynicism as a result. They can, however, predict the climate with considerable accuracy. That is because the climatic forecasts are a result of many weather readings meticulously recorded over hundreds of years.

When choosing a climate in which to live, we would not be deterred by last week's weather forecast. The weather in Melbourne, when considered over a long period of time, becomes a sensible and reliable *climate*. This is despite the days of bitter cold or sweltering heat often seeming so unpredictable, particularly in regard to the exact date of occurrence.

If we had a long-term frame of mind — in other words, if we looked at the *investment climate* instead of the *speculative weather* — none of the above would be an issue. Many of us are paralysed by our perceptions of the past. Some of us agonise over investment decisions each week, yet these decisions are merely some of the many investment decisions we will make during our lives.

Most of us begin our working lives with very little accumulated wealth. We accumulate our wealth in the course of our working lives. Inevitably, we will make many decisions over the ensuing years as we accumulate the wealth required to ensure a stable and worthwhile retirement. We need to stop agonising over the short-term decisions like: Is this the right time? Will the market fall in the near future? What if interest rates rise?

We need to ignore the short-term *static* and choose the most appropriate asset for the longer term. Invest and then look forward to the next opportunity to invest. We should stop looking backwards.

Superannuation is a prime example of what we should do with the rest of our money. Under the present superannuation rules, we can't access the money until we are at least 55 years of age (for some even older). We can't fiddle with it and it has to stay there for the long term. People do not gather around the coffee machine in the office each payday discussing whether or not it is a good time to put their monthly superannuation contribution into international or Australian shares. It is enough that we have established ourselves in a superannuation program.

We should take the same view with our discretionary savings and simply substitute years for months. Invest this year, next year and the year after with the confidence that the prices we pay for assets today will be forgotten by the time we reach retirement. (Think about the family home, and the price it cost thirty years ago. You might have paid $20,000 for that home, and at the time you probably thought: I hope we can afford it. Thirty years on, the house will have increased in price to $250,000 – $300,000.)

If we give ourselves enough time, our investment decision simply comes down to picking the most appropriate asset to invest in. It is your choice, but make a decision now, before it is too late.

CHAPTER FOUR
THE COST OF SHORT-TERM TIME FRAMES

When it comes to deciding about investments, setting goals is important, but having a timeframe for those goals is just as important.

Look at the graph on page 19; it shows the income stream from an investment of $100,000 in two types of assets (shares and term deposits). Examine the graph and decide which is the more attractive.

It doesn't look too hard a task. The lighter shaded bar clearly seems to provide the more attractive income stream. For many people, financial decision-making revolves around a three-year time frame such as this. It is not the norm to contemplate the distant past or the future when trying to decide what to do with our money today. Many of us are too busy to give a great deal of thought to these matters or to do comprehensive homework.

We base our decision on our most immediate experience lumped together with whatever prejudice and perceptions we have acquired. Many of the prejudices we have acquired about investment will have come from our parents initially, and later from our peer group. For better or worse, many of our financial decisions rest on our perceptions and the experience we have enjoyed during the current year, the previous year and our expectations for the coming year. We are relying on the *weather* for our financial future.

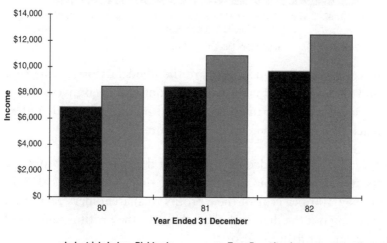

Income Return on Investment of $100,000

We tend to look at our income performance over a relatively short period — like three years. This comes from our habit of viewing assets one dimensionally. If we now stretch the time frame to something more meaningful, we get a totally different picture. The two income streams in the graph on page 20 come from two assets that usually lie at opposite ends of the investment spectrum.

The light shaded bars are the interest payments that would have been received if $100,000 had been placed on a 12-month term deposit and rolled over every year. The income is spent each year and the original capital is simply rolled over for a further 12 months.

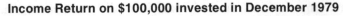

Income Return on $100,000 invested in December 1979

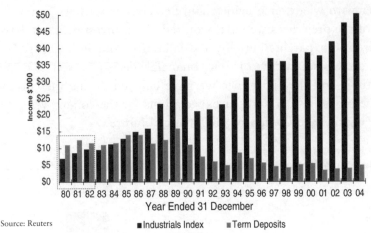

Year Ended 31 December

Source: Reuters ■ Industrials Index ■ Term Deposits

By contrast, the dark shaded bars are the dividends or income that would have been received if the same amount had been invested in a basket of industrial companies, represented by the Industrials Index. (Refer back to Chapter One if you are unsure).

The dividend or dark shaded bars represent that part of the profit the directors feel it is prudent to pay at that time. Companies do not normally pay 100 per cent of their profits to shareholders each year, so after paying out the dividend, the balance of the profit is reinvested into the business for future growth.

In the example above, at no time has any of the income been reinvested in either account, so these income amounts represent only

Industrial Shares versus Term Deposits
Investment of $100,000 in December 1979

	Term Deposit	Shares
Total Income in 25 yrs	$210,025	$660,645
Last Income cheque	$4,750	$53,098

Source: S&P ASX

one dimension of these two assets. All of us could have invested in these two income streams over the last 25 years.

Before continuing it is important to acknowledge that term deposits have a role to play. They are there for savings — for the short and medium term goals we have. For example, house deposits, holidays, minor emergencies and so on. As an investment, however, term deposits should not even appear on our climatic radar.

THE INCOME AND GROWTH FALLACY

Let's discuss the first of many contradictions that appear, because the investment industry tends to simplify such matters to the point of confusion. Historically we have classified term deposits as *income* investments, because of the high yields and stable asset base. Shares, on the other hand, are normally classified as growth investments and not purchased for income. The yields on shares are generally low and most of us try and profit from the share price fluctuations. For many, the hope is that the share price fluctuations will be up, not down. This is trying to predict the weather.

Over the longer term, the total income from shares is far superior to the interest payments on term deposits. This apparent contradiction will surface again and again, and for precisely the same reason on each occasion. In the current context, the contradiction occurs because our time frame for setting the rules is short; when applied to a longer time frame, the rules reverse. In the short term, the income from term deposits looks attractive, but once the time frame goes out to something reasonable (10 years or greater), the income from industrial shares is far superior.

Despite the popular myths, I use shares for income, not growth; and I use term deposits for nothing. For many of us it is counter-intuitive to consider shares as an income source. Tradition would suggest these low yielding investments fail to offer a strong source of income. We never question the popular beliefs, and as a result, we only ever see half the picture. I call this the yield *trap* — an issue I will take up in a later chapter. However, this trap leaves us buying and selling shares in an attempt to make money quickly, whilst ignoring the major reason why share prices grow over the long term. We become short-term speculators instead of long-term investors, even if we started with the right intentions.

Before leaving the graph below we should deal with an anomaly. The dividends (dark shaded bars) for 1988, 1989 and 1990 are much higher than the previous years and then they appear to drop before beginning to rise again. The reason for this untidy appearance is simple. In those years, Paul Keating, the then Treasurer of Australia, made some fundamental changes to the tax system. In June 1987 he introduced Dividend Imputation. The removal of the double taxation of dividends by this piece of legislation was partly responsible for the *hike* in dividend payouts by Australian Companies in the 1987-1988 Tax year.

Income Return on $100,000 invested in December 1979

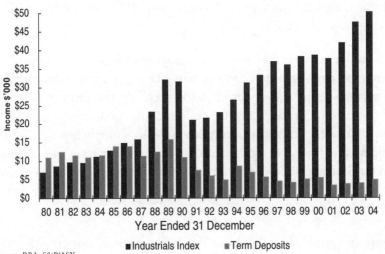

Source: RBA, S&P/ASX

Tax changes also affected performance in the following years. This time, the reduction in corporation tax from 49 per cent to 39 per cent; subsequently it dropped to 33 per cent, was later raised to 36 per cent, and is now 30 per cent. The dividends were again raised temporarily by this change. With the cuts in corporation tax, companies were now paying their dividends with Imputation Credits at the reduced corporate tax rates; however, many companies still had 49 per cent tax credits in their A franking accounts. Sensibly, they opted to get them into shareholders hands and the only way they could do it was by paying *special* or third dividends; (companies normally only pay two dividends a year). This resulted in much larger total dividend payments in years 1989 and 1990.

These tax changes were the cause of one-off dividend spikes and should be ignored in the context of the ongoing income stream. If we average out these special payments we get a more accurate picture of the long-term trend of dividends from Australian Industrial Companies (see graph below).

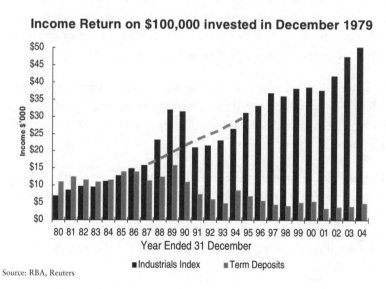

Income Return on $100,000 invested in December 1979

Year Ended 31 December

■ Industrials Index   ■ Term Deposits

Source: RBA, Reuters

If we can now look at the graph in its totality, I would pose the following question: Are you comfortable with the trend of the dividend bars over the long term?

While you contemplate your answer, let me make some apparently outrageous statements. As an investor, I cannot cope with the volatility and the *risks* involved with term deposits. I prefer the safety and security of the share market! This is an apparently contradictory statement in light of our very narrow view of these two assets. Let me add another: as a potential retiree, I look forward to the boring predictability of shares in my retirement!

In the two previous sentences there are four words: safe, secure, boring and predictable. These are not words one normally associates with share investing.

The reason I use them is simply because I follow income streams (dividends), whilst everyone else follows share prices. They watch the prices changing hourly, daily, weekly or yearly.

They have palpitations as their fortunes wax and wane with the price fluctuations suffering the vagaries of the weather. I sit, bored witless, choking on my dividend cheques each year enjoying the climate. The amusing part in all of this is that we are both looking at the same asset; it's just that we have different perceptions.

This is where our *one-dimensional* view of assets brings us undone. We follow prices, which are driven by sentiment and speculation in the short term, whilst the dividends deliver a major part of the value to shareholders.

Whether we like it or not, we continue to judge our wealth creation progress on the short-term price movement of everything we own, with little regard for the income potential.

Stupidly, the illiquid assets, which appear to lack volatility, give us the most comfort.

Just keep this in mind: assets are two-dimensional (i.e. they generate income and have a value) and we ignore either one of these dimensions at our peril.

THE TWO-DIMENSIONAL PICTURE

The following graph shows the second dimension or value of a term deposit and the Industrials Index over the last 25 years. If we look at price alone, the volatility of shares is highlighted and the certainty of term deposits reinforced.

Return on Investment of $100,000 - December 1979

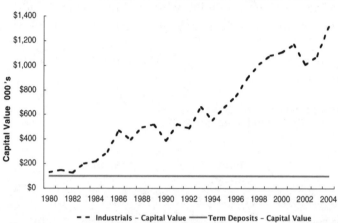

Source: Reuters

On price alone, my $100,000 investment is worth the same 25 years later (and I have ignored inflation). The $100,000 in shares however, is worth just over $1.3 million.

Return on Investment of $100,000 - December 1979

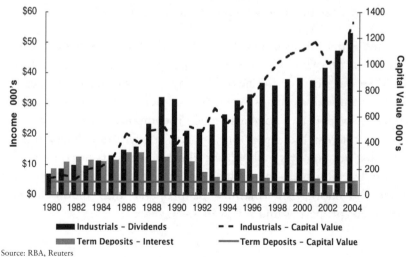

Source: RBA, Reuters

25

We have already examined the income streams from these two asset classes over the same time period. If we place both graphs together for the two-dimensional picture, as shown on the bottom graph on page 25, some important visual images emerge.

Firstly, there is a strong relationship between the income and the value of these two quite different assets. The term deposit asset base is flat and the income fluctuates around it, whilst the income from industrial shares grows over time and the asset base fluctuates around the income.

This two-dimensional relationship is the most important link in judging the TOTAL value of an asset.

Industrial Shares versus Term Deposits
Investment of $100,000 in December 1979

	Term Deposit	Shares
Total Income in 25 yrs	$210,025	$660,645
Last Income cheque	$4,750	$53,098
Final capital value	$100,000	$1,322,280

Source: S&P ASX

To understand how perceptions often interfere with our view of reality, consider the following mind experiment:

I am the Prime Minister and I have shut the Stock Exchange. It now only opens on one day a year. On this day, we can all rush in, trade, and then buzz off for the next 364 days. We will no longer see the prices of individual shares being flashed across our TV or the front page of newspapers. I have also made it compulsory for house prices to be run across the top of our TV screen every day. Every finance journalist now reports daily on the likely movements in house prices, suburb by suburb. As a result, many people become so concerned about the short-term volatility of property that they sell their investment properties and invest in SAFE shares.

Under such a system, shares would look solid, and housing prices would seem incredibly volatile. In other words, it is our perception of certain aspects of the financial system — fueled by the way movements in prices are reported — that causes us to see the share market as a risky and volatile form of investment.

Accept for a moment the scenario I have suggested above; the annual movements of the All Ordinaries Index would look like this.

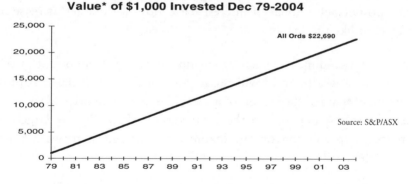

Australian Shares
Value* of $1,000 Invested Dec 79-2004

As I perceive things differently, the chart below is my view of the same period.

Australian Shares
Value* of $1,000 Invested Dec 79-2004

A couple of things are worth noting: We have all arrived at the same point. The difference is that I have chosen to ignore all the daily *noise* that passes for market intelligence.

In reality, there are only two days when you know what a property is worth: the day you buy and the day you sell. Everything in between is useless conjecture. I have simply applied these property rules to my shares and, like property owners, ignored all the useless conjecture in between!

Returning to the two-dimensional relationship: it is best described by using two terms associated with public companies — the *dividend payout ratio* and *retained earnings*. These are descriptors of two elements of most successful companies. Most public companies do not pay 100 per cent of their profits to shareholders each year. Normally, a part of the profit is paid as a dividend to shareholders, and the balance is ploughed back into the company. It can be used for new plant and equipment, research and development, new technology or acquisitions.

If a company trades profitably for five, ten, fifteen or twenty years, and each year it pays part of the profit to us as a dividend, and retains a part of its profit, what is likely to happen to the asset base of the company? Naturally, it would grow; therefore, in the graph at the bottom of page 25, the dark shaded bars are the part of the profit paid to us in dividends each year whilst the balance, retained earnings, are reflected broadly in the dark line. To complete the comparison above, in my terminology, the term deposit has a 100 per cent payout ratio, and as you do not put a dollar of interest back into it, it doesn't increase in value, unlike the shares.

It is this two-dimensional relationship that is most important in the creation of wealth and I will revisit this concept a little later. A final comment: part of the reason that the industrial share price (dark line) is so erratic compared to the term deposit (light line) is largely a matter of perception or our inability to distinguish between price and value.

The price of these businesses is quoted daily and can fluctuate wildly. Most people, whilst watching price, would have no idea of the value of these same businesses. It is only in the longer term that the true value of these shows through. In other words, we tend to worry about the weather instead of enjoying the climate.

CHAPTER FIVE
THE PARABLE OF JILL AND COLIN

In the changing investment environment facing us, it is worth examining the basics of wealth creation. The high inflation years of the 70s and 80s have created a mindset that ignores the basic requirements of long-term wealth creation — i.e. thrift and financial discipline.

Thrift and discipline — they're old fashioned terms. Two generations ago the importance of thrift was unquestioned. Thrift was a key focus of the folk wisdom of the times; our grandparents would say: 'Look after the pennies, and the pounds will look after themselves.' They were tough times, and people needed to save carefully and be cautious about how they used their money.

I would like to remind you of the overwhelming power of these two factors and the potential for all of us to create substantial real wealth. To do so, we will follow the fortunes of two individuals. You could call this a parable.

Colin and Jill have much in common. They share similar aspirations and follow similar careers. Their personal lives are also similar, but the waxing and waning of their fortunes are very different. Their aspirations, when we first meet them, are probably much the same as those of many 20 year olds — they're sort of nebulous. Both want to get rich, do exciting things and live satisfying lives.

However, there are subtle differences, even at the outset. For Colin, it is important to look wealthy from day one!

At the age of 20, they are both working and earn $25,000 p.a. after tax. They both purchase cars. Colin's image requirements translate into a $35,000 purchase price. Jill's more practical requirements are met with a $20,000 purchase price. Colin knows he must save and commits $125 per month to a savings account with a bank. Jill, with an eye to the future, settles on a higher savings goal; in addition to this $125, she saves the difference between the cost of her car lease and Colin's.

We revisit Colin and Jill at age 30. During that period their salaries have risen to $35,000 p.a. net and they both have accumulated savings in investment accounts that have grown at 6 per cent p.a. Colin, with strict budgeting has accumulated $20,485 and Jill, with her higher savings has accumulated $68,365.

They are both struck by the nesting urge at the same time and go house hunting. They have had it drummed into them by their parents that nothing beats property as a means of wealth creation — it's a must for the retirement nest egg. Ever image conscious; Colin opts for an *Entertainer's Dream* that has caught his eye. Jill, practical as ever, has found a modest house that fits a long checklist she has drawn up; she wants a house that is close to parents, allows her to shop conveniently, is near theatres and so on. Colin's purchase price is $200,000 and he uses his savings to pay a deposit and cover costs. He thus borrows $180,000 at 9 per cent. Jill's savings reduces the purchase price of $150,000 and she therefore only borrows $85,000 at 9 per cent.

Whilst both are very conscious that savings are important, Colin is now heavily committed; but he still feels it necessary to have a car that looks good; one that fits his image of himself. Jill too maintains a car similar to the previous ones she has owned. Colin's commitments now preclude him from saving, but he is confident that he is building assets for the future.

Jill is perhaps more conscious of debt than Colin because of the very old fashioned attitudes of her parents. In addition, Colin's parents have tacitly encouraged him because of their very positive experience with debt and property during the 70s and 80s and are convinced it is the right way for him to go.

It is at this point that significant differences appear.

Colin commits to a 25-year mortgage with repayments of $1,511 per month. Jill, nervously taking on a large debt in addition to her other commitments, opts to repay her loan at a higher rate. (It is equivalent to Colin's $1,511 *PLUS* the difference between the cost of her car lease and his.) She is keen to further reduce the debt quickly. Hence her repayments are at the rate of $1,803; as a result, Jill's debt is expunged within 5 years. Once the debt is cleared Jill sensibly commits her mortgage repayments to savings and is pleasantly surprised and comforted by how quickly they accumulate.

Their positions as they enter their 40s looks like this and we begin to see the significant divergence.

	Accumulated savings	Home Loan outstanding
Colin	$0	$148,844 (11yrs to go)
Jill	$125,795	$0 (paid off 5 years ago)

Further salary increases see them start their 40s earning $45,000 p.a. net.

Nervousness with debt forces Colin to re-examine his position and he increases his mortgage repayments from $1,511 per month to $1,760 per month. Although they are both committed individuals, it is during this decade that they both marry. At the age of 50, their different lifestyles and different strategies are beginning to have a huge impact on their wealth creation prospects. They end their 40s in very different financial positions.

	Accumulated savings	Home loan outstanding
Colin	$0	$24,285 (1 yr to go)
Jill	$565,179	$0 (paid off 15 years ago)

The years pass, and the big day arrives for Colin: he retires from the company he has faithfully served for over two decades.

	Accumulated savings
Colin	$541,187
Jill	$2,050,084

Colin was a respected and popular member of the team and had established a reputation as a larger than life individual who was honest and hard working. True to form, Colin acts decisively to put his affairs in order. He is quietly proud of the savings he has accumulated and invests this amount to produce retirement income. Unfortunately, his parents' influence still pervades his thinking and he places his $541,000 on term deposit yielding 8 per cent and is pleased to see that he is now receiving two thirds of his pre-retirement income ($43,000 p.a.) from that term deposit.

True to form, Jill retired quietly. Her savings of $2,050,084, invested in quality shares yielding 4 per cent, provide her with an income of $82,000 p.a., growing steadily, just as it had during her working years and whilst she was reinvesting them. She has now stopped reinvesting and with income splitting, Jill and her husband enjoy a virtually tax free income thanks to dividend imputation. Contrast this with Colin, whose income of $43,000 is fully taxable.

Is there a moral to the story?

There are in fact several. If we wish to create wealth we need to follow some simple principles:

1. We need to save on a regular basis, and place those savings in investments which yield real returns. In other words, we need to find ways to make our assets work for us.

2. We need to spend our money cautiously, not over-committing ourselves, and thus facing high levels of debt repayment. In other words, we need to ensure that our liabilities are as low as possible. When we do take on debts, they should be for investment, not consumption, and we should repay them as rapidly as possible; being in the wrong kind of debt retards the creation of wealth.

3. We need to be clearly aware of our priorities, and be willing to make short-term sacrifices in order to achieve longer-term goals.

4. We need to be informed, so that we can make informed decisions. We need to understand notions like assets and liabilities, to understand the workings of various investment possibilities as well as the ever-changing workings of the tax system.

5. And finally, we need to develop a clear strategy, and that strategy needs to be long-term.

CHAPTER SIX
TAX AND INFLATION — THE SUBTLE ENEMIES

In the previous chapter, Colin was heavily influenced by the investment habits of his parents in the 70s and 80s. Let's look more closely at how his parents lived.

Inflation is an insidious enemy. It appears to be our friend while often destroying our lifestyles. During the 70s and 80s salaries rose sharply, as did house prices. This was the *friendly* aspect. What was disconcerting for many was the flip side. Prices rose and the cost of living skyrocketed. However, interest rates were also high during this period — and this was a double-edged sword.

For those living on interest income in retirement, 14 and 15 per cent term deposit rates were superficially attractive. However, after such people had paid tax on the interest at around 30 per cent, they ended up with a net 10.5 per cent. When we then subtract the rate at which prices were increasing (approximately 11 per cent) they were actually going backwards — but perceptions were that times were good.

The second of our two enemies was tax. When tax rates are perceived to be too onerous they create biases. The tax system in this country produced some very strong biases until Paul Keating introduced major reforms in the mid 80s. Capital Gains Tax was introduced in 1985. Prior to its introduction the message from the tax system was simply this: if we could produce a speculative profit or capital gain, we were given a pat on the head and we paid no tax. If, however, we went to work to earn a living, or produced rental, dividend or interest income, the Taxation Office clipped us over the ears and took up to 66 per cent of our income away.

Following the introduction of Capital Gains Tax in 1985, Paul Keating introduced dividend imputation in 1987. With these two changes, he effectively turned the tax system on its head. Now we paid tax on capital gains at the top marginal rate, and imputation removed the iniquitous double taxation that occurred when company dividends paid to shareholders were taxed — a system that had applied for decades.

People have been slow to respond to these far reaching changes. Old habits die hard, and attitudes developed over many decades mean that our investing habits remain based on the out-dated tax system. We still prefer asset accumulation to income generation. Negative gearing is a prime example of this.

Negative gearing became very popular during the period immediately prior to these tax changes. Negative gearing is based on the premise that we give up the income from an asset because we pay more interest on the loan than we receive in income. We make this sacrifice in the hope of a capital profit at some time in the future.

Neutral gearing is where the income from the investment matches the interest bill; and positive gearing is where the income from the investment exceeds the interest cost. Enough books have been written on this topic, so I don't intend to turn this chapter into a lesson on how it works.

The most common asset for gearing was property. We simply borrowed a large sum from a bank and purchased an investment property. Normally the interest we had to pay would exceed the rent that we received, so we would have to subsidise the interest by paying from other income. This additional income that we gave up was not subject to tax, so we effectively used pre-tax dollars to pay the bank. We gave away a dollar to avoid a 50-cent tax liability. Naturally, the result had to be good to justify this sort of behavior. We believed the payoff would come when we sold and the profit would more than compensate for the income we had forgone.

GEARING IN THE CURRENT CLIMATE

When property markets are rising and have not delivered a disappointment in six years, negative gearing is considered a quick way to riches. The term *negative gearing* has become ubiquitous and many people use it without fully understanding the implications.

To be negatively geared, the interest cost of the borrowed money must exceed the income generated by the asset purchased with the borrowed funds.

For example: You purchase a property for $175,000 as an investment, and borrow $150,000. At a 6 per cent interest rate, such a loan would require repayments of approximately $1000 per month. The rent for the property however, is only $600 per month.

This then enables the borrower to spend other income to make up the interest shortfall. By paying this money to the bank as interest it becomes a deduction from our income before being assessed for tax.

For many this is the major attraction. Pay lots of your income to the bank and avoid paying tax on it! The payoff comes when you sell the asset for a capital gain and (theoretically) recoup all the income paid to the bank.

For many, the whole concept of negative gearing has become blurred: Is negative gearing used for its tax benefit or is it to increase wealth?

Depending on who is giving the advice, the reason for gearing could differ. Some clients are advised: 'You're paying too much tax, you should gear.' Or, 'You need to make money quickly as you are retiring soon — you should gear.'

There are parallels here between the investment practices of individuals and those of a business. Many businesses continue to run modest levels of debt on their balance sheets. Most of these businesses can invest the borrowed funds and generate a return greater than the net cost of the interest they have to pay. For an individual this would be called gearing, for a company it is called good business.

The important element here is the level of debt. I use the word modest to describe current debt levels for industry. We only have to go back to the 80s to be reminded of how even good businesses in the wrong hands can overdo the debt. Bond Corp, Quintex, Ariadne, Adsteam and Elders are just a few that fell victim to, among other things, high debt levels!

If the borrowings are to enhance our long-term return, then the debt levels should be modest and sustainable. Any over-gearing will leave us vulnerable to either a plunge in asset values (margin call) or a hike in interest rates (income squeeze). When property markets ran hot and notional interest rates were low, gearing was perceived to be a licence to print money.

I would like to offer an alternative view. Gearing is a means of sensibly leveraging long-term investment returns. The major factor in wealth creation is time. A modest amount of debt in the most appropriate asset will over time seriously enhance our wealth and thus, our options in life.

To better grasp the role of time to the equation, consider the graph on page 38. If we had borrowed money over the last 25 years to invest in Industrial equities, our borrowing costs would have approximated to the light shaded bars in this graph. If we had put the borrowed money into an industrial share fund, the investment result achieved broadly reflects the capital performance and dividends, illustrated by the dark shaded bars and the dark line on the graph. This graph assumes a 100 per cent gearing level, which is neither prudent nor possible for most of us. However, it does illustrate the long-term benefit of gearing. Borrow the light shaded bars and invest in the dark shaded bars!

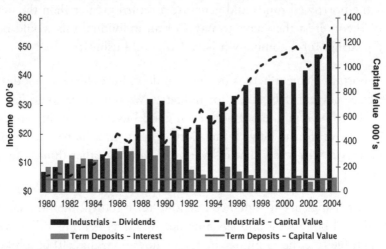

Return on Investment of $100,000 - December 1979

Source: RBA, Reuters

Many people believe that it is a good idea to gear property because you can borrow 100 per cent, and sometimes more. This reflects attitudes, not commonsense.

Few people realise that you can also negatively gear in order to invest in the share market. Income from property reflects the bulk of the return during a period of low inflation. Also, during these periods, house prices do not rise as sharply, so borrowing up to 100 per cent of the purchase price and thus negatively gearing doesn't make sense. You are unlikely to recoup all the interest costs incurred if the price of the property doesn't increase. If gearing allows you to run faster in the wealth creation stakes, running in the wrong direction (i.e. wrong asset class) isn't going to help.

Why the strong emphasis on property? The major reason is that during the 1970s and 80s, inflation gave the Baby Boomer generation the illusion that their wealth was growing. We borrowed money, bought a house and two things happened: inflation DEVALUED the debt and INFLATED the price of our houses. We told our friends — and ourselves — that we had bought our house for $20,000 and it was now worth $200,000. It gave us a feeling of achievement. We chose to ignore the fact that the worth of every other house in our neighbourhood had increased by about the same extent. OUR house had gone up by the most, hadn't it?

There were other structural reasons for this focus on property. Most lending institutions in Australia would only lend against real estate and these same institutions rarely make a margin call on property that has fallen in value. This attitude is still prevalent today, although changing. However, it has left us with a legacy of comfort associated with debt against property and discomfort with debt against other assets or cash flow.

Clearly, all this worked well during the period of post-war inflation, when asset prices rose automatically and the value of debt was automatically reduced. The combination of a skewed tax system and inflation has given rise to an entire generation of Australians who are liability rich and income poor. In many cases they live in a relatively large and expensive house and cannot afford to eat very well.

Let us examine the impact of inflation a little further, as this has been one of the key post-war influences on our investing habits. We tend to have a love–hate relationship with inflation. On the one hand, we are always complaining about the rising prices of goods and services; on the other hand, very few complain about their house price increasing.

During this post-war period of high inflation, house prices rose and the value of our mortgage was reduced. The longer we owed money on the house, the better.

Inflation would eventually wipe out our indebtedness and ramp up the price of our house. This however gave us a false sense of security; the truth of the matter is that inflation, whilst pushing up prices, did not alter the VALUE of the property. This meant that if we wanted to sell and move to a similar house in either the same neighbourhood or a better one (this was the norm as we rarely trade down in neighbourhoods) we had to pay the same or more. So whilst house *prices* rose, rising house *values* were an inflationary illusion.

Where we actually made the money was in the devaluation of our mortgage. We never actually repaid the debt; we just waited for inflation to destroy it. We have managed to translate the devalued mortgage into making money out of property. The fact that we could have done better with exactly the same borrowing by investing in good businesses instead, is only now beginning to surface in the awareness of investors. The rule for baby boomers during the inflationary decades was: borrowers win and lenders lose.

What happens if we don't learn from history?

Let's look back. An advertisement caught my eye in 1989. The story behind it is a salutary reminder to us all. It came out of the Coles Myer 1989 Annual Report. They were doing a retrospective on the company. The headline was '21 piece tea service, 2/6d.'

The comment that caught my eye was part of the caption attached to the photo. It read: '**Coles sold nothing over 2/6d from 1914-1939, when inflation made the limit impractical.**'

Inflation was the key word in the caption. My mother could pop a penny into a jar each month until she had saved the 2/6d to buy the tea service for her glory box because for 25 years there was no inflation. During this period of 25 years, there was zero inflation; the period also included a depression, when the longer you owned a property, the less it was worth.

This was a very different paradigm to the one that now pervades our society. We should acknowledge that tax and inflation have been two of the biggest drivers of our money attitudes, and both have changed dramatically. In a period of high inflation, borrowers win and lenders lose. During periods of low inflation, lenders win and borrowers lose. Debt is not devalued over time and property prices do not rise as steeply.

It is instructive to look at industry to appreciate this lesson. During the 80s, industry was happy to borrow despite the fact that interest rates for borrowings were at 17 per cent or more. This was because they were able to take advantage of the outcomes mentioned above. Contrast that with today where industry generally is largely equity funded with modest levels of debt. This is because industry understands the high *real* cost of money in the current environment. In the past, when interest rates were at 13 per cent and inflation at 10 per cent, your real cost of money was only 3 per cent. With interest rates at 6 - 7 per cent, and inflation at 3 per cent or lower, the real cost of money today could be as high or higher than periods during the 80s.

Paradoxically, we are presently being encouraged to borrow ever more as the advertising tells us that interest rates are low. That may be true of the nominal or headline rate of interest, but the REAL cost of money is high. From an investor's perspective this is good news, but must be treated with caution. Interest rates have been reduced regularly in most countries as governments desperately try to avoid a *hard landing* for the global economy.

The flipside of this is that at the first sign of a recovery, governments fearful of a resurgence of inflation will lose no time in raising rates as aggressively as they have reduced them. This is the game of chicken that is played between governments and speculators on a global basis. As governments try to protect their economies (us) from our speculative excesses, they create a moral hazard. That means many of us tend to speculate even further in the knowledge that we will be rescued. Eventually someone will miscalculate and the inevitable head-on will occur. But remember, the government is a *Mack truck* in this game.

SENSIBLE BORROWING MAKES SENSE!

I do not want to leave you with the impression that I am against all borrowing. Not at all.

Industry still carries debt on its balance sheet. Why? Because a MODEST level of debt is a sensible practice for most businesses.

This is in contrast to the immodest levels of debt that were prevalent in the 1980s. The debt can be used to smooth cash flow, increase stock levels during periods of short-term high demand, and so on. The important point here is that most businesses make the decision to borrow based upon their ability to produce a rate of return on the borrowings greater than the net cost of the borrowed funds. If the return on the borrowings is LESS than the cost of the funds, the debt will drag the company backwards.

If we as individuals wish to use debt sensibly, we should only use borrowings for investment purposes, not for consumption. And we should ensure that the rate of return on the borrowed dollars is greater than the net cost of those dollars over the long term. More importantly, we must rely on the performance of the asset, NOT inflation as we did in the past.

GROWTH DOES NOT EXIST!

Negative gearing relies on the *growth* in an asset to make the scheme work. The problem is that growth doesn't exist! Growth exists in the organic world, not in the inorganic world. You grow, I grow, plants grow — but money doesn't grow. Yet we persist in describing assets as growth assets, when in fact they NEVER grow. Inflation may raise the price of an asset, but does not necessarily increase its value. A simple rise in price does not mean it has *grown* despite the illusion.

Ultimately, what gives an asset value is its income stream. A term deposit that pays no interest would attract few investors. A property with no tenants or rental income, or a business that generates no profit, would have little appeal for sensible investors. What gives an asset sustainable value over the long term is its ability to produce an income year after year, and if the asset is to increase in value, then part or all of the income must be reinvested back into the asset. Then, and only then, will the elusive *growth* be achieved.

Although inflation gave us a *perception* of money growing, the only thing that happened was that the price of our house went up, but its VALUE didn't change.

Let me see if I can demonstrate this *double standard*. Assume we purchased a house in 1970 with borrowed money. Let's say the mortgage was for 20 years. During that period, the rate of inflation was high and this devalued the debt. What this meant was that we never really repaid the debt; we simply waited for inflation to demolish it. Over that same period, high inflation pushed the price of the house ever skywards.

Having paid off the house in 1990, we place it on the market as we wish to move to a similar house, but in a nicer suburb. What price will we pay for this new acquisition? If we're lucky, the sale of our old house will deliver enough to allow us to purchase the new house; it is more likely, however, that we will have to take out another loan. It is important to understand that for most people at this time, not only did they move to a nicer suburb but also inflation driven salaries meant that they could now borrow even more for the next house and thus buy even bigger.

Although the price of our original house went up, the value hadn't changed at all. All the other properties around us went up at roughly the same rate. It was the steady increase in the amount of debt that we were prepared to accept that drove our fortunes. As I mentioned previously, debt is a winner during periods of high inflation as it is steadily eroded over time.

It is interesting to look back at the first house we purchased in London in 1975. I agonised over the purchase price of £15,000 pounds and the huge loan of £12,000 pounds that was used to fund the purchase. I shouldn't have worried; inflation took off over the next 5 years and by 1980 the retail price index in the United Kingdom doubled. Salaries shot up, so that when I sold in 1982 and moved with a new job the loan had become a joke and the sale price of £60,000 pounds looked terribly clever. Guess how much I had to pay to buy the next house? In real terms, we have never moved ahead in the ownership of property despite prices moving ever higher.

To increase the value of an asset over the long term, two things must occur. First and foremost, the asset must produce an income stream. Secondly, a part or all of the income must be reinvested into the asset to increase its value. If you want a term deposit to grow, reinvest some of the interest. If you have purchased an investment property and from the day it is bought, you spend nothing ever again on the house, it will eventually fall down. Barring one-off rezoning or redevelopment, unless money is poured back into a property it will decline in value, even though its price may go up. If you want a business to increase in value you must reinvest a part of the profit. When all the income generated by an asset is spent or withdrawn, in most cases, the asset will eventually die.

A recent development in this area has been the Property Investment clubs that have sprung up. Seminars are run pushing a message most people want to hear and believe: *property is the only true road to riches*.

The natural *speed limit* for property remains our ability to pay for it. As a result of the high inflation during the 70s and 80s, our ability to pay was increasing rapidly as incomes shot up. Property prices spiraled upwards with incomes.

The current irrational exuberance has been fuelled, not by increasing salaries, but by a massive increase in debt. This misallocation of the productive capital of Australia, and other countries, has drawn the attention of economists around the globe.

Like all bubbles, this one will burst. It will happen when the *bubble* has reached its point of maximum expansion. In the case of the property bubble, it will occur at the moment when almost everyone believes the outcome is a *sure thing*. Only then will the truth eventually surface. Regrettably, because of the sheer size of the debt burden and the lack of liquidity that property possesses, when the inevitable occurs, it will be painful for many.

As much as governments may have wished to prick the bubble before it became life threatening, their hands have been tied. Raising interest rates would have choked the speculation. But with one eye on fragile economic recoveries and one eye on the boom in property, they sit and hope.

CHAPTER SEVEN
WHY BUSINESSES PAY DIVIDENDS

When a company is successful, and makes a profit, its directors may choose to pay a portion of the company's profits to shareholders. This is called a *dividend*.

Shareholders hold conflicting views about dividends, and their attitudes tend to depend on their age and employment status. Those who are working do not require the dividends; people in this group favour the company retaining more of the earnings and boosting the share price. This lightens the tax burden on the shareholder. The tax slug will only arise on the eventual sale of the shares by the shareholder.

From a purely theoretical tax point of view this probably makes sense under the present tax regime, but there are a number of practical problems involved with this approach. A company will not alter its payout ratios just to suit the requirements of individual shareholders; when the shareholders require income, they must sell the shares and invest in a dividend paying company. The potential capital gains tax liability would make a big hole in the retirement savings of any investor.

Secondly, if a company is trading profitably and not paying dividends, then franking or imputation credits would pile up, undistributed to shareholders. These credits are enormously valuable to shareholders. Retirees take note: you currently receive the full value for these credits whether you pay tax or not.

A NOTE ABOUT FRANKING

If you are a new player in the investment field, you may find terms like *franking* and *imputation* credits a little confusing at first. Let me explain these terms through an example: Imagine that you have $10,000 to invest, and you're trying to decide between two potential forms of investment, both of which offer a 4 per cent return on your money. One is a term deposit; the other is shares that are franked. Which yields the better return? The naïve answer is: 'Neither — both yield a 4 per cent return.' But let's look more closely.

The dividend from your investment in shares carries with it a franking or imputation credit. This simply means that the company has *already paid* Corporation Tax (30 per cent) on behalf of its shareholders — and this works very much to your benefit as an investor.

Look at the following chart:

	SHARES	TERM DEPOSIT
Income	$400	$400
Plus imputation credit	$171	0
Total taxable value	$571	$400
Less tax @ (say) 40%	-$228	-$160
Add back Imputation Credit	$171	0
Net tax payable	-$57	-$160
Gross income	$400	$400
Net tax payable	-$57	-$160
Total income after tax	$343	$240

Retirees should favour the payment of dividends, as this strategy provides the most favourable income stream for their lifestyle. Sadly, too few retirees take advantage of this strategy. The problem is one of perception: they believe the constant fluctuations of prices means that such investments are insecure. They also assume there won't be sufficient income initially.

How are we to resolve this dilemma? How can we meet these conflicting requirements? The answer lies in the middle ground. Above all else, the management of the company must set the payout ratio with the best interests of ALL shareholders over the long term. For some companies with limited capital requirements, the payout ratio can be high. For those with heavier capital needs, the retained earnings will be higher.

Let's return to the situation of people already earning an income — that is, the group that prefers a lower dividend. Although superficially it would appear sensible to retain earnings to boost share price growth, there are inherent dangers with this strategy. Deferring dividends means that the reward to shareholders is held back, till some unspecified point in the future. There is a hidden assumption in here, and the assumption is that the management of the company can do better things with ALL the money than you, the shareholder, can do with some of it.

Dividends are not just cash payments. They give the shareholder a reward for providing the risk capital and liquidity for the enterprise. Nowadays, share options often form part of an incentive package for employees. This often leads to a very overweight position in the shares of our employers.

Let me explain this more simply. I worked for one of Australia's top 20 companies. They had a policy of issuing shares to staff in lieu of bonuses and as a mechanism for holding salaries down. (These shares were, in fact, another form of deferred remuneration.)

Many staff had worked with the company for many years, and had accumulated huge shareholdings in this company. Many also reinvested dividends every year. The company enjoyed steady growth in dividends and share price.

Recent management decisions have seen the company's share price halve. If staff had diversified across other businesses, by taking their dividends year after year and reinvesting elsewhere, the impact of this sharp fall would not have been anywhere near as painful.

I often hear the argument that companies paying dividends could suffer from a shortage of capital, hindering future growth. Some *spin-doctors* for United States investment banking companies argue that paying dividends is like an admission that the management of the company has nothing better to do. This is wrong on two counts.

Firstly, the tax rules in the United States are very different from those in Australia. They have no dividend imputation (although this is currently under discussion) and they enjoy concessionary Capital Gains Tax regimes. Secondly, industry has always been able to raise capital successfully to fund expansion. It is perfectly logical for a company to pay out sensible dividends, whilst retaining sufficient profits for normal operations. If an opportunity arises that requires additional funds, then a *rights issue* of new shares to raise fresh capital is a sensible option.

A *rights issue* could occur where a company decides to acquire another business. For example, *company A* is capitalised at $1,000 and has 1,000 shares on issue. All things being equal its share price would be $1,000 divided by 1,000 shares — that is, one dollar per share.

Let us assume *company A* decided to acquire *company B. Company B* is capitalised at $500 and had 500 shares on issue. *Company A* has no excess capital, so goes to existing shareholders with a *rights* issue to raise the capital for this acquisition. They offer existing shareholders one new share for each two that are held, at a price of one dollar.

On the basis of one for two, the existing 1,000 shares in *company A* will raise $500 for the acquisition. There will now be a total of 1,500 shares on issue; *company B* disappears into *company A*, which now has a capitalisation of $1,500 and a share price of $1,500 divided by 1,500 shares equals one dollar per share.

Apart from anything else, the *rights issue* enables shareholders to closely scrutinise the proposed acquisition or expansion, and to decide, through their vote, whether to take up the new shares.

Contrast this to a company that retains more profits than necessary and then finds itself under pressure to do something with this *lazy capital,* and in haste makes a poor decision without reference to shareholders. This pressure may not come from the marketplace itself, but may be imposed by a board or chief executive who, impressed by the size of the bank balance, buys for the sake of buying.

You can never stop a rich fool from paying too much!

Worse than this, Enron and Worldcom are superbly sad examples of share price growth at all costs. Accounts can be manipulated to provide an illusion of share price growth. Dividends, by and large, must be paid out in cash.

Today, industry in Australia generally is very well capitalised. Some businesses have returned capital to shareholders, as they have not been able to usefully employ it in the business.

This return of capital has taken two primary forms: share buybacks and special dividends.

As a result of this activity, the question emerges: what is the point of a company retaining profits in an attempt to allow shareholders to avoid income tax when the company has absolutely no use for the capital?

The market punishes companies that have retained earnings and accumulated *lazy* capital on their balance sheets. The market pulls their prices down and management is punished for not doing something with the excess capital.

Secondly, the theoreticians are correct: there is in Australia, a marginal benefit at the moment for those taking capital gains as opposed to income.

The practical difficulty with this is that share prices are volatile, whilst dividends generally are not. If an investor must rely on cashing shares for income, then income streams will become equally volatile, providing many opportunities for regret.

This is not a practical solution — neither for retirees, nor for income seeking investors in general.

CHAPTER EIGHT
A BASIC BUSINESS MODEL

The education system in this country seems designed to create wage slaves; it is certainly not geared to produce entrepreneurial free thinkers. I picked up most of my financial habits from parents, friends and hard experience. The education system is slow to change. When I was invited to speak at my sons' school, I used the following simple example to get across the basics of business value to his math's class.

Imagine a small family business, one that produces lemonade and sells it at the local market. The table on the opposite page shows the progress of this small business. It's a modest enterprise.

We started the business with initial capital of $100, which was used to buy an old trestle table, an Esky, plastic cups and juice squeezers. As prudent business people, we modeled the business and we found that, all things being equal, at the price we planned to sell the lemonade, we would generate a return on our capital of 10 per cent. In year one the business ran like clockwork and we generate a 10 per cent return. Voila! We have a $10 profit.

Year	Assets	Profit R.O.E	Dividend	Retained
1	100.00	10.00	5.00	5.00
2	105.00	10.50	5.25	5.25
3	110.25	11.00	5.50	5.50
4	115.75	11.60	5.80	5.80
5	121.55	12.20	6.10	6.10
6	127.65	12.80	6.40	6.40
7	134.05	13.40	6.70	6.70

We must now set our payout ratio, which is the amount of the profit to be paid out to shareholders. Looking around at other businesses, we discover that payout ratios can vary considerably. In the end we adopt a 50/50 split, similar to the current BHP Billiton ratio over the long term. The shareholders — my wife and I — enjoy an immediate dividend of five dollars, with the balance of the profit ploughed back into the company as retained profits or earnings. We used these retained profits to upgrade the juicer — we wanted one that let fewer pips through — and we are going to phase in glasses instead of plastic cups — our customers told us they would prefer this.

This wise use of the retained profits enabled us to increase our profit in Year 2 — again, a 10 per cent return on the now expanded assets. This meant a slightly higher profit. When split 50/50, this yielded a slightly higher dividend than the previous year. This pleased the shareholders and also enabled us to make some further improvements with the higher retained earnings.

Year 3 went according to plan, as did Years 4, 5, 6 and so on. Despite the seeming oversimplification of this example, this is about as complicated as business gets. Shareholders subscribe capital that generates a return. The shareholders are rewarded with a dividend, and the balance of the profit is ploughed back into the enterprise. The business trades at a profit in Year 2 with shareholders again receiving a dividend and the balance of the profit being ploughed back and so on.

It is the underlying concept that is important. Share prices and dividends of good businesses rise over the *long term* for perfectly rational reasons. A lack of understanding of this simple concept causes much of the fear associated with investing. If we do not understand this process, it is easy to become anxious. The thinking goes something like this: if share prices and dividends rise over time, then they could just as easily fall, couldn't they? The liquidity of the market provides the short-term volatility (the weather) and feeds into this anxiety; the next step is to see investment in shares as risky (and meteorologists as fools).

TREATING YOURSELF AS A BUSINESS

What is true for business is true for individuals. Each of us is a business in our own right. We each have a *net tangible asset value*. In my case, it is the amount my life is insured for. If anything happens to me, my wife receives a one-off lump sum payment ($100) as a capital replacement for my future income. Thankfully, she hasn't tried to bump me off in order to receive the lump sum. However, every year I put my *capital* to work as an employee of a company and I generate a return on my capital. It is called a salary or wage.

Let's assume that I pay my family a dividend from this profit (salary) amounting to half. We live on this and I retain the other half of the *profit*. If I invest the *retained profits* (in every day life we call these *savings*) wisely, it will increase my profit (income) slightly in Year 2. If we live on half and I save the other half and invest it wisely, it will increase my asset base for Year 3 and so on.

Consider this parallel in a little more detail. Write down what you think your *net tangible asset value* is. Then work out what your return on equity is (i.e. how much do you earn in total each year?). Then work out your dividend payout ratio or, looked at in another way, how much do you spend each year? This will leave you with your retained earnings or savings. Finally, look at how you invest those retained earnings. Do you buy assets or liabilities? Having created your *company profile,* compare your corporate performance against some of Australia's best companies, and see how you stack up. I have no doubt that many of you will not measure up to the best business practices.

As you can see from this analogy, the rule remains the same for wealth creation, irrespective of whether you are a company owner or an employee. Don't spend all you earn and if you can do it for long enough, you run the grave risk of becoming wealthy! This requires discipline that for many of us is sadly lacking and the substitute becomes speculation. For many, the adage is: 'Today's pleasures beckon more strongly than tomorrow's pain.'

A *BAD* BUSINESS

In the previous example we looked at a simple model of a good business, well run. Now we will consider a good business badly run, using the same template.

At the end of year one, my wife and I are summoned to our accountant's office for the end of year *reckoning* for the tax office. The accountant advises us that he has bad news. We are dismayed. 'What is it?' we ask. He replies, 'You have made a profit and will have to pay tax.' We agree that it is bad because we have been led to believe that you must do all in your power to avoid tax.

We ask him if it is possible to avoid tax and he indicates a scheme involving planting some exotic tree that will make our fortunes. In the meantime, the amount we put into this planting will be a tax deduction. In the end we opt to lease a new, very large and expensive imported car. As the lease is also a tax-deductible item, we get rid of the profit and pay no tax.

If you refer to our model, we now have no profit, no dividend and no retained earnings. However, we do have a large and expensive car. This means that we start Year 2 of our business with the same $100.

If we again generate a 10 per cent return on the capital, we have a profit of ten dollars. If we are again successful in *burying* the profit to avoid tax, as in Year 1, we again have no dividend and no retained earnings.

The company starts Year 3 with an asset base of $100. Clearly, if this goes on the value of the business is unlikely to increase as the retained earnings are nil and the profit and dividend stream are also unlikely to increase. Whilst we may enjoy an enhanced lifestyle initially, our future prospects are bleak.

As it is for business, so it is for us individually. If we spend all we earn and save nothing, we also have no future.

THE *DOTCOM* BOOM

If we combine elements of poor business practice with *irrational exuberance* we end up with something like the *dotcom* boom. Let's trace how this scenario works.

We start a business called Lemonade.com with $100 capital. We don't actually have a business at this stage; it is nothing more than a concept. We end Year 1 with no profit, no dividend and no retained profits. In fact, we spend $30 of the company's capital marketing this amazing concept.

The company then starts Year 2 with only $70 capital remaining. Again, we end up with no profit, no dividend and no retained earnings. What do we start Year 3 with? Only $40. Clearly this is unsustainable. Don't misunderstand me, some successful businesses are incubated for many years before they become profitable; it's called development or venture capital. It is very high risk and specialised — an area for the experts only. When we start pushing these into the public arena, as new floats or IPOs (initial public offerings), greedy amateurs create a recipe for disaster.

Second only to irrational exuberance in the wealth destruction stakes is that time of year when a young man's fancy turns to thoughts of how to avoid paying tax. Here is a brief trip down memory lane for anyone contemplating sure-fire tax minimisation projects. This shame file is presented in no particular order of merit.

One of my favorites is the *Tropical Oyster Co Pty Ltd* fiasco of 1993. The company was going to grow oysters in Indonesia. There were two big selling points: firstly, the promise that any expenditure associated with viewing or attending meetings in Bali or Lombok *should* be tax deductible; secondly, that 80 per cent of the subscription price was guaranteed as a loss in year one.

Next, is *Afro Ostrich Farms Ltd*. The advert for the ostriches is a classic of its kind: 'You can gain a tax deduction and pay off your house in under ten years'. How? 'Just one pair of Afro Ostrich chicks will do it'. The promoters sold the idea that responsible parents **owed** it to their children to buy them a pair of chicks. 'Build your family's wealth with Ostriches,' trumpeted the ads. The ostrich industry was forecast to produce $180 million each year in Australia.

Emu farming became fashionable in the mid 90s, with similar disastrous consequences. Even the Americans got into the act. The following quote is entertaining. 'Emus in the United States have an investment history that the directors of Bre-X Mining and its shareholders would recognise. In 1993, pairs of breeder birds were fetching somewhere around US$35,000 and up to US$70,000. As everyone dived in, the market glutted and today the same birds are worth US$1,000 to US$3,000'. But what a great tax deduction!

Headlines such as the following began to appear: 'US emu farmers kiss their nest egg goodbye' and 'Cracks appear in emu's golden egg'. There were many bizarre twists to the emu saga. One farmer in Texas who, frustrated by the losses he was incurring, began to club the birds to death. Faced with an animal that had gone from being the golden goose to being an albatross, hapless owners were keen to get rid of them, but the slaughterhouses were turning them away. In the late 90s, news reports reached Australia of law enforcement officers pursuing feral emus across the Texas plains; their owners had let the emus loose, rather than meet the costs of feeding them. By this time, a pair of breeders was on sale for only a few dollars!

Next comes the *worm farms*. One Victorian company provided a 10 kilogram bucket of worms and a growing kit in return for $3,000 and the possibility of earning more than $15,000 per year. One worm farm promoter took $2,850 from 500 investors. Prices quoted for worms was the equivalent of three to four times the price of prime rump steak!

A scheme that still appears is the *Cricket Bat Willow Plantation*. Projected returns of 17.4 per cent per annum net and 100 per cent tax deduction were on offer.

Some may remember the ASIC-sponsored advertisements for *tax effective* schemes. These included: *geeps*, a cross between goats and sheep; the *Millenium Bug insurance scheme*; *bluebottle farms*; *land and air space packages*; and others.

So for those who are still disappointed with investment returns, here is a chance to make amends. You could invest your money in one of the *sure fire* opportunities offered every June that promise spectacular returns with fabulous tax benefits. Just don't expect any actual **investment returns**.

CHAPTER NINE
THE YIELD TRAP

This chapter requires your focused attention, because the concepts are quite complex. You need to be able to hold two separate dollar values in your head, as well as the abstract (yield) relationship that they have. Please persevere, as this is an important part of the story.

Thus far, we have looked at the two-dimensional nature of assets. We are now going to look at these two elements together mathematically. If we divide the income from an asset by the value of the asset we get the *yield*. For example, if a bank account has $100 invested in it and at the end of the year you receive a cheque for ten dollars interest, the yield is 10 per cent. (This is another example of the bad habit of trying to simplify things and reduce them to a *one-dimensional* view.)

I can hear you say, 'Why are you telling us what we already know?' For the uninitiated there is a trap in this simple calculation. When retirees seek income in retirement, they seek the highest yields. People assume that high yields and high income is the same thing. This may be true in Year 1. However, this is not true in the longer term. Why? Income is an ongoing need for most of us, whilst yield is a *spot* figure calculated at a point in time.

From the graph below we can plot the yields over the 25 years by simply dividing each interest payment by the value of the term deposit, and multiply by one hundred. For example, in the year 2000 we could have obtained 5 per cent on term deposit. To calculate the yield perform the following calculation:

$$\frac{\$5,000}{\$100,000} \times 100 = 5\% \text{ (the yield on the term deposit)}$$

If we do this each year, we can plot the yield of our term deposits over the 25 years on a graph. If we do the same with the Industrials Index (i.e. divide the dividend each year by the value of the portfolio), we can plot the yield on the Industrials Index over 25 years.

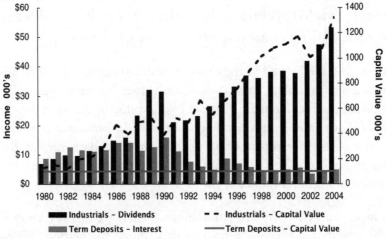

Return on Investment of $100,000 - December 1979

Source: RBA, Reuters

In the graph below we can see the yield comparison for these two assets.

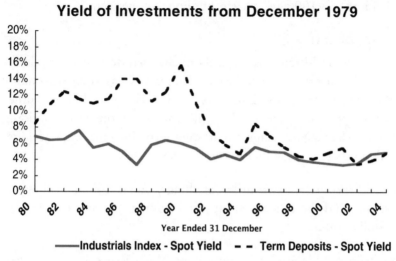

Yield of Investments from December 1979

Year Ended 31 December

———Industrials Index - Spot Yield   – – Term Deposits - Spot Yield

Source: RBA, S&P/ASX

Clearly from the yield graph, a person seeking income during the 80s would have opted for term deposits. It is only in the latter part of the 90s that the gap between the two yields narrowed. Over the longer term, the yield on the Industrials Index has been relatively flat. This has meant that for 25 years at least, people seeking income would have chosen term deposits over shares for two reasons: Firstly, because there is a perception that cash deposits are safer than shares; and secondly, because the yield on term deposits was greater.

Let's now dig a little deeper. The reason the yield on Industrial shares is relatively flat is because the dividends rise over time and the value of the businesses or the share prices do the same. If we are dividing one value (dividend) that is rising steadily by another value (share price) that is rising steadily, we end up with a constant called *yield*, which over time changes very little.

For example, if we look at the dividends and value in 1980, we find that shares at that time were yielding approximately 5.5 per cent ($\frac{\$6,900}{\$132,180}$ x 100). In 1993, the dividend of roughly $22,960 divided by a portfolio value of $661,860 gave a yield of 3.5 per cent. In 2004, the portfolio value of $1,320,288 million divided into a dividend of $53,100 gave a yield of about 4.0 per cent.

THE YIELD TRAP

Although the yield remains virtually unchanged over time, the dollar value of the income from industrial companies has risen reasonably steadily since the investment was made. The paradox for other investors appears to me in the following way: the lower yielding Industrial shares pay magnificent long-term income; high yielding term deposits pay lousy long-term income!

Yield and *income* are two different things; one is a dollar value you can spend, and the other is an abstract number or ratio that has no clear dollar value.

The reason yield is used is because it simplifies issues at a time when we are making a decision. Many people find the explanation difficult to comprehend, because they must hold the mental image of two dollar amounts (value and income) plus the *abstract* yield.

In simple terms, *yield* is a number; it defines the relationship between the value lines and the income bars as shown in the graph on page 60. The higher the value lines relative to the bars, the lower the yield. Conversely, the lower the line relative to the bars, the higher the yield. Because the value of industrial shares (line) remains close to and synchronized with the bars, the yield remains persistently low.

If you look at the graph in the period 88 - 90, you will notice a large disparity between the value (line) and the income (bars). In these years, the *yield* was clearly large, whereas in the years prior to 1988 and after 1990, the *yield* is low.

People make an income choice at a point in time without the benefit of knowledge or much thought for the future. Choosing term deposits as a sole or major source of retirement income requires that we die quickly; otherwise, we may live long enough to regret the decision.

HIGH OR LOW YIELD?

Previously I have made the statement that I prefer *low yielding* shares. I should explain what I mean by this. I make this statement to draw a distinction between the yields on two different asset classes. If, however, I am looking at shares alone, then some basic rules must be taken into account.

As I mentioned earlier, yield is an abstract derived from two absolute dollar values. So, for example, a one-dollar share paying a 5-cent dividend has a yield of 5 per cent.

$$\frac{5 \text{ cents}}{100 \text{ cents}} \times 100 = 5\% \text{ yield}$$

The two variables that will affect the yield are:

1. THE PRICE OF THE SHARE
2. THE DIVIDEND PAID

If the dividend is relatively stable and increases steadily over time we would expect the yield to increase if the share price remained flat. As we have seen from the earlier chapters, the share price generally also rises over the long term, and as a result, the yield remains flat.

So much for the theory! We know from experience that share prices are subject to quite wild fluctuations in the short term as a result of speculators betting on these short-term movements, changes in sentiment, *tea leaf readings* and so on.

If our theoretical company has a bad patch and analysts downgrade the short-term profit outlook, it is perfectly feasible that short-term players could sell the stock and with no immediate buyers the share price will fall. Let us assume that company management is comfortable with the longer-term prospects for the company and that they maintain the dividend. (This is generally the norm as would be apparent from the long-term stability of dividends displayed in my previous graphs).

If the share price were halved under strong selling pressure to 50 cents, and the dividend was maintained at 5 cent, the yield for this company could, in the space of a few weeks, jump to 10 per cent (i.e. five cents divided by 50 cents multiplied by 100). This is a result of a change in one of the variables in the yield equation.

So, whilst I am comfortable with *low yields*, I am also happy to buy a *high yield* when it is the result of a stocks price falling due to short term selling. Warren Buffet put it beautifully when he stated: 'The share market is a mechanism for transferring wealth from the impatient to the patient.' This occurs when a good business is subject to short-term selling pressures by people or institutions that have no knowledge or understanding of the business itself or the environment in which it operates.

Clearly, the opposite could apply. If the share price doubled because punters believed the stock had great potential, then the yield would halve to 2.5 per cent. This fits my criteria for a low yield, but it is important to understand why the yield is low. Is it because the share price has run way ahead? Am I paying too much today for the future income? As I mentioned earlier, it is holding these key concepts in our minds and creating the appropriate images that often proves difficult.

The hard part for a time-poor DIY wealth creator is knowing whether a share price is artificially inflated or deflated. Has the management of the company revealed all the facts? Will the dividend be maintained, cut or increased? And most importantly, of all the shares quoted, which ones should you focus on?

In 2002 we enjoyed a rare bonanza. With share prices tumbling with little regard to value, and dividends rising, we could obtain a higher income by buying bank shares than lending them our money on term deposits.

At the time, I was a buyer of higher yielding shares, simply because prices were being hammered.

WE MUST BE HONEST WITH OURSELVES

This is where outsourcing becomes a vital part of sensible investment. We shouldn't kid ourselves that we can develop the necessary knowledge and expertise, and make the appropriate decisions in our spare time. Whether we like it or not, fund managers have a role to play in performing this function, and good advisors have a role to play in helping us select the most appropriate funds and managers for what we want to achieve. If you have decided to become a long-term investor, your choice of fund manager must be made carefully. It is important to remember: some fund managers will speculate and churn a portfolio of shares more than we ever could. Despite their self-promotion to the contrary, some fund managers speculate more than most would-be investors. Paying for appropriate advice ensures that we get the funds and managers needed for us to invest in the future.

CHAPTER TEN
WHAT WE REALLY DO WHEN WE SELL

Let's return to the graph on page 67. Not only does it display the two characteristics of the primary assets — income and value — it provides a three-dimensional picture: it includes *time*. This gives us some interesting insights, as we rarely include this factor of time in our decision making.

Consider the following possibility. We retired in 1980 and invested all our retirement savings in industrial shares. My wife and I decide to go on holiday in 1986 and we are gone until 1988. We rent a broken down villa in Tuscany. It is central and our globe trotting children can leave the grandchildren with us during school holidays. Upon our return we discover there was a *crash* in 1987.

Undisturbed by all of this, we go away again in 1993. This time, we rent a cottage in Devon. We do not return until 1995 and again we discover that there was a financial market meltdown in 1994. With the benefit of hindsight, it is interesting to look back at those periods and note how clearly the drop in share prices is reflected in the graph. It is important to note that because of our one-dimensional view of these assets, it was the fall in prices that affected the sentiment at the time; panic was widespread amongst the punters.

Return on Investment of $100,000 - December 1979

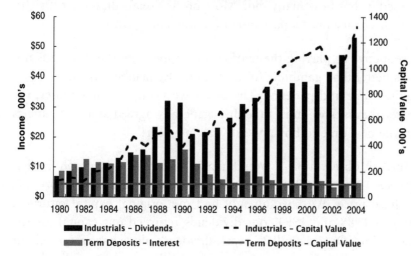

Source: RBA, Reuters

Having plenty of leisure time I am able to consider the graph and notice one thing. Although the prices of shares dipped in 1987, our dividends rose. Although the value of our portfolio dipped in 1994, our income rose. It should not go unnoticed that during the Dotcom bust in 2002, as share prices fell, our dividends rose again. It is this stability of income that gives us comfort in retirement. The value of our portfolio, whilst not irrelevant, is of little importance on a day-to-day basis. I have lost nothing by not selling. In fact, the people who lost the most were those that did sell as they panicked and fled.

In the current uncertain climate it is worth examining our feelings regarding this issue again. Despite all the uncertain sentiment at present, we are feeling comfortable with our results just as we have during the past periods of turmoil.

I have no doubt that clever friends would counsel, 'Yes, but if you were smart and sold before the drops, you could have bought back in at the lower price.' Wise advice! And normally, such advice is offered only with the benefit of perfect hindsight. How many people have the expertise and the time to do this? Who will pay the capital gains tax bill? This is the *get rich quick* syndrome. Of course we could have finessed it, but how many did? Most professionals didn't get it right, so what chance does a part-time rank amateur have.

As seductive as playing the market may appear, market timing is not much better than gambling for most of us. Remember, wealth creation requires time and patience. The faster we want to make money, the greater the risks we must take. It is generally agreed amongst experts that the best time to buy and sell was last year!

A further observation I would make regarding this graph is that between 1980 and 1988, the dividends are equivalent to our original purchase price. We have already had our original capital returned. Between 1988 and 1991, our dividends returned our capital for the second time. Over the full 25 years, dividends alone have returned our original capital over *six* times, and we still have our portfolio that is now worth around $1.3 million. Dividends in the current year now represent a yield of over 53 per cent on the original investment and this is in an environment where a 6 per cent yield looks attractive.

THE TRAP FOR RETIREES

It is sad to watch many retirees take their superannuation when they retire, and despite having invested reasonably sensibly during their working lives, they now go ultra-conservative. They cash up and then invest in term deposits for safety. They would have held shares in their superannuation fund during their working life, and then they undo the good work just when they need shares the most. What they don't seem to realise is that when they cash up, they convert all the future dividends they will never receive into a lump sum.

As time passes, the risk with shares diminishes. When we diversify, our capital is returned in dividend payments and any short-term fluctuation in our asset base is a *non-event*. Our lives are now secured and many options become available to us.

CHAPTER ELEVEN
UTILISING CAPITAL AS INCOME

Utilising capital as income has always been a legitimate strategy for some investors; however it is a forced outcome for many who retired too early with too little. It is worrying to see that this strategy becomes more widespread when bull markets are running.

As we come to accept rises in share prices as the norm, so we build *new* strategies around these perceptions. We are presently being told that the halving of the capital gains tax has meant that it is marginally more efficient for shareholders to take profits as capital gains by selling shares, rather than the company distributing them as dividends.

The theoretical model is sound, but I suspect many will struggle with the implementation, leaving aside the fact that for many decades, whilst there was no Capital Gains Tax in this country, many Australian companies still paid dividends to their shareholders. This is despite the fact that much of Australian industry was resource-based and thus in no position to pay dividends.

Today, the bulk of shareholder wealth in Australia comes from manufacturing and service industries, most of which have paid dividends for many years. I have touched on this issue in some detail in previous chapters. I now want to address some of the more practical aspects of this.

From earlier graphs, it is clear that the one stable aspect of investing in good businesses is the *long-term growing income stream*. For some Australians this had provided certainty and peace of mind in retirement. Despite the *theoretical* attraction of capital consumption, I think it is fair to say that most of us do not completely optimise our portfolios. In fact, Modern Portfolio Theory (MPT) tells us that to *optimise* our investments, we should hold a minimum of around 60 per cent of our assets in overseas shares. We all know this is the optimal solution, but I do not see optimised portfolios for many investors! Prejudice and fear override theoretical optimisation.

In many instances, it is impractical to rearrange our affairs each time there is a change in tax legislation just to optimise our portfolio. So for most of us, we drag along with theoretically sub-optimal portfolios. Remember that, for most of us, the single biggest impact on our long-term wealth will not be the tax structures we use, but the asset class in which we invest.

Retirees suffer most from capital consumption. Should they no longer rely on dividends? Should we tell them that selling shares would give a marginally better result? I believe this will provide more opportunity for regret. Many investors endure regret and, even worse, the *fear* of regret.

Which shares should they sell? When is the right time? What if the market is flat? Should they wait until it comes back? What if it doesn't? Advisors will, no doubt, offer a range of quite different solutions. Which advisors will be right and how do you choose them?

Consider the graph below. This plots the price of News Corp shares over the calendar year 2000. They started the year at $14, rose to $28 and ended the year at $14 again. As News Corp virtually demands that you cash in shares to collect income (the dividend is paltry), how many opportunities for regret did investors have in 2000? Although not included, the charts for 2001 to 2004 look perilously similar. What's changed? Not much! When should we cash in?

Daily price of News Corp Ordinary shares in 2000.

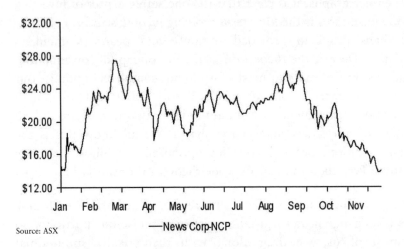

Source: ASX —News Corp-NCP

We need to look closely at the affects of the *selling your assets* approach on retirees. This group of people had enjoyed stable and growing income from their share portfolios (that required little if any maintenance) and we have now forced them to confront regular buy or sell decisions — the last thing they want to focus on in retirement. We have replaced this stable income with the consumption of potentially erratic capital. All of this is just to display how clever we are as an industry in providing *theoretically* correct models to a constantly changing tax environment.

As an industry, we encourage people to utilise dollar cost averaging (i.e. regular investment) during wealth creation to overcome the worries created by volatility, as we put our money away for the future. With the regular cashing in of capital for consumption — that is, dollar cost averaging in reverse — we bring the volatility of prices right back into focus.

Allocated pensions are currently a source of concern to many retirees because of this issue. These pensions require considerable expertise to structure correctly so as to ensure that the effects of regular withdrawals does not destroy them prematurely.

As often happens, the theoreticians are in love with the model and most people will hopefully ignore perfection and make do with what is practical.

CHAPTER TWELVE

DO ALLOCATED PENSIONS HAVE A DESIGN FLAW?

Many allocated pension clients have been witnessing an alarming fall in their asset base as they cash-out bigger and bigger unit holdings to maintain the dollar value of pension payments. Too often, allocated pensions are sold on the basis of their tax treatment, not on the basis of an understanding of investment fundamentals.

It is important to remember what an allocated pension actually is. An allocated pension is an investment designed to provide an income stream over the investor's life expectancy. (The *life expectancy* of a person is estimated on the basis of a range of factors: current age, sex, and so on.) It is also important to remember that they are designed to run out.

The income or pension is paid from the earnings of the investments held in the product. Generally the product provides reasonable levels of flexibility in terms of where monies can be invested. The important thing to note is that it is the investor who takes all the investment risk. With annuities, which were a traditional source of income for retirees, the issuer or insurance company took all the risks and guaranteed the income for a lifetime, however long that might be.

It is ironic that one of the criticisms of annuities was their lack of flexibility. People didn't want their capital to disappear on death. Well, welcome to the real world where there are no free lunches. You want flexibility and you also want to retain control of the capital? Well you can, but did you remember to ask the price of such a *package*.

When a client starts an allocated pension, you would normally place around the equivalent of the first two years income payments into cash. A planner should do this to limit the initial impact of any short-term market fluctuations.

But what happens after the end of this two-year period? This depends on where the money has been invested. If the investments have been placed into total return style funds, then come the end of the two-year period, the client's pension payments will be at the mercy of the short-term and long-term market fluctuations. Arguably, the cash account should have been replenished during this time by cashing in some or all of the increases in unit prices that occurred during the first two years. If this were to occur, a problem may not arise - at least not immediately! However, if there hasn't been any growth, how does one replenish the cash account?

What do I mean by *total return funds*? Most managed funds are Total Return. There is little distinction (indeed, often no distinction) between income and unit price growth. The managers do not look at these components, merely the overall reinvested result compared to a benchmark. Any *income* paid from the fund is usually a combination of realised gains, interest, dividends, and so on. After fees it can be a big or small amount and is largely dependent on the level of trading activity undertaken by the manager.

The net effect is that whenever a pensioner wants to take a pension payment, he or she needs to cash-out some of their unit holdings. Often a planner may have placed the client in a range of asset classes and would be seeking to take pension payments from the more conservative portfolios in the early years, such as cash, fixed interest or capital stable. It should be noted that with a balanced fund, you do not have control over which asset class money is drawn from.

I mentioned the need to avoid market fluctuations with the first two years pension payments; it's obviously important to do this over the long term with these products. What can happen over the first two years can happen over the life of the product – remember it is you, the investor, who is taking the investment risk at all times.

The problem is that some clients seem to have their allocated pensions nearly fully invested in Australian or International shares or *growth* assets. And, as markets go down, so does the value of their unit holdings. There is no growth to cash-out for the legislated *income* payments. At the same time there is possibly little cash investment to use.

In effect what's happening is *dollar* cost averaging in reverse. Investors are cashing in a smaller number of units during good periods, but a much larger number of units during the down times. Clients have been relying on asset price growth and a few morsels of income earned within their fund, reflected in the account balance, to act as a substitute for actual income payments. As has been sadly demonstrated, the increases in the account balance can evaporate more quickly than it accumulated because you have two negatives hitting it at once … one is the negative share or unit price; the other is the pension payments. Mathematically, two negatives are supposed to make a positive, but this doesn't apply in this instance.

In an ideal world, an allocated pension should always be holding the next two years income payments in cash. What is important, at a minimum, is that the fund should have a reasonable expectation of receiving sufficient income to make most of the actual pension payments over the next two years.

For obvious reasons, this requires an approximation to be made about likely income receipts. Naturally, this should be determined on a reasonably conservative basis. As the construction of an allocated pension is predicated on the eventual rundown of the capital, we have to draw that process out as long as possible. The occasional dud market is going to accentuate the capital draw-downs anyway.

As you have been reading this book you will have become increasingly aware of my overwhelming preference for shares. So doesn't the requirement to have this cash buffer show up a flaw in my thinking? Remember, the issue here is not the quantum of exposure to growth assets. The issue is how much income is being generated by the assets to make pension payments.

Assets held in an allocated pension must generate income. It is impossible to rely on steady growth, as it does not occur with all assets. My personal allocated pension will hold at least two years cash when I decide to kick it off. During that two-year period I will receive income, (which might be dividends, interest, rent and so on) which will continually replenish the cash account from which pension payments will be drawn.

I intend to always have the buffer there, as I hate the thought of being a distressed seller in duff markets. I'm not going to undo the habits of a lifetime! More importantly, my allocated pension is only PART of my retirement income strategy. It is not the be all and end all, as is the case with some advisors. Allocated pensions are income products and the underlying assets must match the product structure and its outcomes. Structurally they are okay but require a different methodology to our traditional view of investing.

It is no use using price fluctuations in assets to produce income short term. This would be alright in the longer term, provided the two-year buffer is in place and is maintained. Clearly, fund manager selection and fund selection is of paramount importance in an allocated pension. Arguably the same rules apply outside superannuation (pension) but because of the lack of flexibility within an AP (that is, the incomes payments are a legislated requirement with strict guidelines for minimum and maximum payments), the fund and manager selection process is more critical.

Investors must be more discerning – by which I mean, more demanding of fund managers and advisors to ensure that they can satisfy clients long-term aspirations. It is fine to have prices drop back as long as there is no income dependence on those unit prices. We all know that long term they will recover but it is of little consolation if the client has much fewer units to recover.

It is no good reducing the draw if there is still no free cash in the fund and the units are under water. The slight reduction in damage is still not going to be appreciated by the investor (pensioner). One of the problems associated with this issue is the fact that a large number of pensioners have become first time and reluctant investors as a result of the growth in defined contribution schemes and the governments push towards income streams as opposed to lump sums in retirement.

Allocated pensions, like superannuation before it, have often been sold on the tax advantages with understanding of, and education about, investment and risk now coming a poor last. Asset allocation can solve part of the problem (just try and remember when Capital Stable funds were discovered to be *unstable*).

The tax advantages have been a great selling point; nil tax environment, 15 per cent rebate, and $50,000+ tax free per couple are all issues which have been repeated ad nauseam. The Centrelink benefits have also been a keen focal point, especially when these products were assets test exempt. In some respects these Government-provided benefits may have helped paper over some of the design deficiencies in the investment area. I wonder if the Government is happy with having performed such a task!

Where recovery times are necessarily short, as is the case with allocated pensions, we must be a great deal more circumspect than we have been in the past. For example, you – as the client – could overcome a poorly designed superannuation contract by switching to a better quality contract and continuing to contribute, provided the early transfer penalties didn't crucify you. This luxury is not afforded to the owners of allocated pensions.

Allocated pensions are a good product. There aren't too many retirees who wouldn't benefit from using a product of this type. The problems I have identified are not issues with the product structure, but with the way some product providers have decided to design and manage these income stream products.

This has not been a problem previously. Allocated pensions really became a mainstream product in 1993 - 1994. In the intervening 10 years or so, we have not really had a sustained downturn in financial markets. Any downturn during that period has been quickly reversed for varying reasons. The downturn in 2002 and 2003 is the first of any significance.

At the same time, Australian investment in International markets had only become more popular in the previous year or two. More recently, the Australian dollar has risen, accentuating losses made on the market.

A number of people have commented at seminars that they were becoming increasingly worried as their allocated pensions were losing value and that they were being forced to consume more and more capital. Although it is no longer a constant topic at every seminar as markets have produced good returns over the last two years, it is not too late to review the strategy you have undertaken as markets will tumble again at some point.

CHAPTER THIRTEEN
MYTHS ABOUT PROPERTY

So far we have looked at two of the primary assets: *productive enterprise* and *money lending*. The third asset is *property*.

We won't look at residential property for a number of reasons — primarily because it is difficult to obtain reliable data for the asset class as a whole. There is also too much emotional baggage attached to residential property and, as most people own a house, it is very difficult to look beyond these issues. I will not sidestep these and will deal with them now rather than allow them to cloud the *investment* issues later in this book. The most common myths are:

1. 'I KNOW PROPERTY'

It is a staggering fact that many people will confidently claim to have some expertise with property. This expertise apparently comes from the fact that they are surrounded by it. Such people follow prices around them and then extend this *knowledge* to property generally.

How many times have we heard someone say, 'Property is looking up. The house down the road sold for so many thousands.' We can then file the information and forget about that price until something else spurs our interest. We remain secure in our belief that the value of the house just sold will not change until it, or another house, sells again.

Many people also make judgments on property values based purely on their subjective view of property. 'I don't know how anyone could pay that much for such an ugly house in that position. Our house would clearly be worth more! It's a nicer house and in a better position.' Having said that, they shut down any further thought regarding property prices in their neighbourhood. We tend to confuse familiarity with expertise.

All in all, most people show a passing interest in property; they glance at the colour photos in the real estate sections of the local paper and — perhaps — dream a little. These are not the thoughts or emotions that regularly run through our lives in relation to shares in Australian businesses. Our house prices do not appear on our television screen every day, reminding us of our foolishness in trying to make a quick buck, or of the highly volatile and unpredictable nature of property prices in the short term.

2. 'PROPERTY IS A GOOD LONG-TERM INVESTMENT'

Ironically it is one of the drawbacks of property that, in the hands of the uninformed, becomes a positive attribute. The lack of liquidity in property (i.e. the ability to sell quickly) gives the appearance of being a positive. Prices are not published regularly; they are not drawn to our attention every day. The lack of liquidity in property means that when sentiment is negative or cash is required in a hurry, a share portfolio is normally the first asset sold or liquidated.

What is a positive attribute with shares for most intelligent investors (their liquidity) becomes a negative in the minds of others. If a property is not performing to expectations, it becomes a case of, 'Well, we will wait until prices improve.' That is, it becomes a long-term investment. The high liquidity of shares (i.e. the ability to buy and sell them quickly) is perceived to be a negative and makes shares risky. Shares are also a great long-term investment when the same rules as those relating to property are applied.

3. 'YOU CAN LOSE MONEY IN SHARES'

The almost infantile assumption that you can never lose money by investing in property should worry people. Indeed, people are actively encouraged to hold this view, despite it being totally wrong. Speculative shares tend to colour peoples' perceptions and, by association, all shares are viewed as being speculative to some degree. The same attitudes are not applied to property. How often have we heard the expression, 'You can never lose money on property'? This does not stop people paying too much for it, and most importantly, totally ignoring the cost of holding it for long periods of time. Although its price may have risen, its value may have declined. Not all property goes up and not all shares go down.

4. 'I HAVE ALWAYS MADE MORE MONEY OUT OF PROPERTY'

This would rank as the least rational of the emotive issues in this whole debate. Normally rational people think nothing of borrowing hundreds of thousands of dollars to *invest in* property, and yet to borrow a modest amount to invest in shares is seen as speculative at best, and foolhardy at worst. If a $300,000 property increased by 10 per cent, an investor has notionally made $30,000. If; however, a $10,000 *punt* on Commonwealth Bank shares doubles in value you have only made $10,000. This faulty thinking becomes apparent again in conversations I've had with many people who claim greater profits out of property because you can gear it more heavily than shares. The logic is seriously flawed, but this view leads to the not unnatural conclusion that you can make more money in property. More importantly, it has not stopped many people from speculating wildly in property, speculation that is masked by the claim that they are *investing*.

5. 'PROPERTY IS SAFE'

Many institutions have reinforced this attitude for decades. They will happily lend 80 or 90 per cent of the value of a residential property but, until recently, very little against share portfolios. Even as institutions rewrite these rules, they still reserve the right to make a margin call, or sell the shares outright in the event that shares fall in price in the short term. How many of these same institutions would make a margin call in the event that the price of a property dropped below valuation? This property margin call rarely — if ever — occurs because all parties assume no one would ever default on property, whilst they would on shares. A look back at the early 90s should remind us of how wrong this attitude is. An irrational splurge on property and property development turned sour and the banks, as mortgagee in possession, became owners of huge chunks of real estate as property speculators went bust one after the other.

6. 'PROPERTY NEVER GOES DOWN'

In two areas in particular, the contrast between shares and property is particularly stark. The first is the lack of a recognised, regular and quantifiable measure of the performance of property. Compare this to the constant reporting of the All Ordinaries Index and all the sub indices, together with the daily listing of the price of every public company. If the prices of all the houses in your street were reported daily, the attitude towards the perceived stability of property prices would change dramatically.

The second area is the language used when talking about share prices. It seems an almost weekly occurrence now; headlines scream out that the share market is *plunging, crashing* or *diving*; perhaps even *melting down*. This hype may be great for newspaper sales and television viewing numbers, but it does nothing for peace of mind. This constant barrage of negative press inevitably has a subliminal effect on our attitudes and perceptions about shares.

Let us now consider four rational reasons for considering shares as an alternative investment to property:

1. REDUCING *RISK* THROUGH DIVERSIFICATION

For most people investing in property, diversifying (or spreading) their investments is difficult. It is impossible for most of us to go and buy 20 properties at the one time. As a result, we often link our fortunes to one property in one suburb, in one city, in one country and one economic cycle. With shares, we can easily diversify initially. With as little as $2,000, we can obtain a stake in many businesses in many countries. If one country suffers an economic downturn, this does not affect the whole portfolio. In other words, it is easy to shield yourself from the short-term ups and downs of the market and remove the stock-specific risks associated with one or more companies going bad.

2. PROPERTY LACKS LIQUIDITY

In the event of a real need for ready cash, it is comforting to know that you hold shares. Once the decision to sell has been taken, cash is available in three days. Some see this positive as a negative. Most people would be appalled at the forced sale of their property, yet accept the forced sale of shares, even though it can result in a negative outcome that reinforces prejudices already present in most of us.

Life has a bad habit of delivering the odd nasty surprise. This is why we insure our lives, houses, boats and cars. We never plan to have something disastrous happen to our families, or ourselves; but from time to time people find their backs to the wall. A forced seller of any asset is unlikely to receive what they think it is worth, and sadly, it is the high level of liquidity and low costs that makes shares the natural first sale for most. Interestingly, people complain about the costs of buying and selling shares, and yet dollar-for-dollar, it costs substantially more to buy and sell property than it does shares.

There are some current *get-rich-quick* books that claim you can make a killing by cherry picking at distressed property sales. Does everyone assume that a distressed sale only happens to someone else and not some hapless *investor*? For every seller there must be a buyer.

It follows that for every buyer who wins, there must be a seller who loses. Not everyone can *win* in this speculative game of buying and selling.

3. TAX EFFECTIVENESS

Many people today still believe that you can only gear property. This in itself is a clear indication of the strong biases at work in Australian society. Gearing is about borrowing money and using it to generate an income. When used in this way, the interest payable becomes tax deductible. Shares, therefore, are a natural for this. Dividends in aggregate are more stable and will grow faster than rents in aggregate. A distinct advantage of shares is that if they are selected wisely, they provide valuable *income tax credits (imputation or franking)* that are not available with property.

Some of the supposed *tax effectiveness* of investment property comes from things like depreciation. I must have missed something, but if an asset is depreciating, that means it is worth less and it will have to be replaced by me spending dollars. Secondly, we can claim a deduction for all the money you pour into it to maintain it. The fact that we have spent the money and don't have to pay tax doesn't make it *tax effective*. We should give our money to charity if that is what we want to achieve.

4. NEW PARADIGM FOR THE FUTURE

We often repeat the emotional arguments about property to our children. In fact, there is an almost pathological desire on the part of most parents to see their children repeat what they have done themselves. Despite the fact that most people will acknowledge the huge changes that have occurred in recent years, they will not accept them in the context of their children's futures.

One of the greatest changes is the greater mobility of capital and technology on a global basis. If we acknowledge that the history of wealth creation has relied on people productively using capital and technology, then it will pay us to understand that our children now live in a global village. Our parents could live and die in one town,

85

often in one house, relying on immobile capital and technology to provide a job for life.

This will not be so for our children.

To succeed in this global village, they must become as mobile as the capital and technology they seek to utilise. We need to encourage them to contemplate the extreme mobility of shares (businesses), and the total lack of mobility of their investment property. Let them understand that overseas they will be able to obtain sensible long-term residential leases, which are just not available in this country. They can enjoy the security of tenure, which most of us desire but cannot achieve in Australia, without the physical ownership. Many of our children will purchase property long before they are *financially* or *emotionally* ready.

A COUPLE OF FINAL THOUGHTS

Bearing in mind the emotional background to our love affair with property, why is Australian industry finally getting property off its balance sheet? They wrap it up in trusts and sell it to an unsuspecting public via listed property trusts. Retailers sell their supermarkets and lease them back. Banks sell their buildings and lease them back.

If property were such a good investment, wouldn't they buy more, not sell it? This tells me that we can make more money running a business than owning property. If the reverse were true, and we could make more money owning property than running a business, why would anyone bother going into business?

If residential property is such a good investment, why doesn't Australian industry invest in it, and why are there no listed residential property trusts that invest in it? Or are we so much smarter than business people? (At the time of writing, a listed residential trust is on the launching pad. It will be interesting to see if it can last any longer than the last one of these, launched many years ago by D. Johnson.)

The answer is: Property is not the lucrative and safe investment we have always assumed it to be. The potential for real wealth creation lies elsewhere.

CHAPTER FOURTEEN
PROPERTY TRUSTS VERSUS INDUSTRIAL SHARES

In previous graphs I have used term deposits and industrial shares to give a sense of the relative value of these assets over time. I now want to include property in this equation, using listed property trusts. Some analysts argue that property trusts do not really represent property, because they are listed.

However, the results achieved by a listed property trust must, over time, reflect the underlying value of the property or properties. It would not be possible for the trust to reflect anything other than that value. In the short term, it is possible that we will see some differentiation, simply because of the liquidity provided by listing the property on the stock exchange and changes in sentiment.

For example, a share has a share price whilst a property trust has a *unit price*. There is no difference between the two; as listed securities they can both be traded up or down.

Direct property holders argue that, because listed trusts fluctuate in value, they do not truly reflect *real* property. This highlights the blinkered attitudes of many to property in Australia. The listing simply provides liquidity for what is often an illiquid asset. To suggest that a property held directly lacks volatility is playing the children's game of, *I can't see you so you can't see me*. Because a property is large and infrequently traded doesn't make it a *safe* investment. The only difference between listed and unlisted is the liquidity that is provided to the listed trust investor and the fact that they don't have to own the whole building as they can buy or sell a part of it.

Whilst that liquidity might produce some short-term volatility, it is only short-term and the long-term trust valuation will remain related to the value of the underlying asset. A direct owner of property may not see any short-term volatility in the price of their property because there is no satisfactory valuation mechanism.

In the graph on page 89, I have separated the income and capital of the Listed Property Trust Index and compared it with the Industrials Index. The light shaded bars (left hand scale) represent the income generated by the CBD office buildings, industrial estates, retail shopping centres, and so on. The light shaded line (right hand scale) represents the value over time of these same properties.

It has always been a source of amusement to me to ask members of the public where they think the value of CBD office buildings, industrial estates or retail shopping centres would be after 25 years. Many believe it would be in excess of the value of the Industrials Index. I then ask the question: 'If you could make more money owning property than going into business, why would anyone ever go into business?' The answer is that more money is made from running a business than from owning physical property. This has been the case for centuries. It just so happens that over the last 25 years many people have had a positive experience with property and, without reference to any benchmark, consider that they have done well.

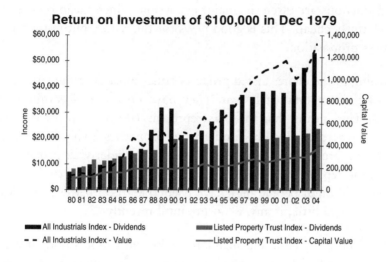

Return on Investment of $100,000 in Dec 1979

Legend:
- All Industrials Index - Dividends
- All Industrials Index - Value
- Listed Property Trust Index - Dividends
- Listed Property Trust Index - Capital Value

Source: Reuters

Industrial Shares vs Property Trusts
Investment of $100,000 in December 1979

	Property	Shares
Total income in 25 years	$421,288	$660,645
Last income cheque	$23,881	$53,098
Final capital value	$367,270	$1,322,280

Harking back to a point I made earlier: if residential property is such a good investment, why was the recent listed property trust, that invests purely in residential property withdrawn because of lack of support? The answer is that there isn't any money in it, so it is left as a *cottage industry*; every man and his dog own a rental property and the industry is inefficient. More importantly, tenants are unable to obtain a sensible long-term lease, and this creates a sense of insecurity, forcing many people to buy rather than rent.

Tax deductions are often the major attraction, which mean that rents are relatively cheap. This is good news for the renter, but not a great business proposition.

Returning to the chart: Listed property trusts must distribute 100 per cent of their income each year. They have no retained earnings or profits. This means that the bars represent 100 per cent of the net income generated by the underlying properties. The line must therefore represent the long-term value of the underlying properties. This graph represents a 100 per cent payout ratio, similar to the term deposit. Although people may have been able to do better in shares, most have had little, if any, exposure until recently.

As direct property comes in such large licks, most of it is bought with borrowed funds. I have covered this aspect of borrowed money and inflation, so will not labour the point. As most peoples' exposure to shares was limited (and almost certainly involved no borrowings), the results didn't ever seem so spectacular. The higher liquidity offered by shares also meant it was easier to speculate. Mind you, the lack of liquidity has not stopped people speculating in property!

CHAPTER FIFTEEN
PROPERTY — THE YIELD TRAP

The yield trap is particularly vicious because property trusts represent a 100 per cent payout ratio. If we refer to the previous graph and ask investors to choose which income stream they would prefer for the long term, investors normally choose industrial dividends.

If we look at the graph over the page, based on the yields offered by these two investments over the same period of time, it is apparent that property trusts have provided the highest yields. These yields, combined with the emotional acceptance of property, has again brought suffering to the unsuspecting. This has not been quite as obvious as the massive drop in interest rates, and for that reason has perhaps been worse.

The situation that prevails with property trusts and yields reminds me of the *boiling frog* experiment. If you drop a frog into boiling water it immediately jumps out. If you drop a frog into tepid water and then gently bring it to the boil, the frog dies whilst swimming around. For many retirees the often-quoted high yields that tend to apply to property trusts give a superficial reinforcement to their desire for *income*. If they were aware of the longer-term implications for their income, I suspect they would *jump out,* or at least reconsider.

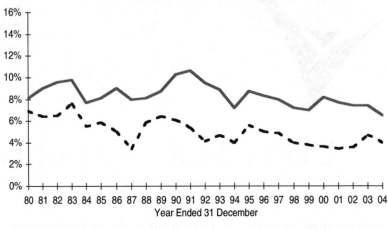

Yield of Investments from December 1979

Year Ended 31 December

———ASX Listed Prop Trust Index - Spot Yield   − − −All Industrials Index - Spot Yield

Source: Reuters

If we return to the graph on page 89 you will see why the yields are high. Looking at property: If we divide an income that is modest (light shaded bars) by a capital performance that is pathetic (light shaded line), what do we get? High yields. Look now at the Industrials Index. If you divide an income that rises strongly by a capital value that also rises strongly, what do you get? Low yields. High yielding property trusts pay poor long-term income; I much prefer low yielding shares because they pay magnificent long-term income.

I argued earlier that growth does not exist. For an asset to increase in value, it must first generate an income, and then a part or all of the income must be reinvested into the asset to increase its value.

If listed property trusts distribute 100 per cent of their income, they will have no retained profits or earnings. If a trust manager wants to buy a new property or refurbish an existing property, they will require cash to do it. They need to either borrow against the existing property or properties, or issue new units or shares. This has the effect of diluting existing holdings. The line graph for property values over the long term reflects this fact. Property requires considerable maintenance and is very cash hungry. We see this in a domestic sense with our residential properties; they cost us all a substantial sum to maintain and upgrade over time, but we often overlook this fact when drawing a comparison with other assets.

CHAPTER SIXTEEN
IF YOU WANT TO MAKE MONEY OUT OF
PROPERTY, DON'T OWN IT

By now, property lovers would be seriously considering ditching this book as so much of what I have written runs counter to what we consider to be common sense. However, I urge you to persist.

At the beginning of the book I talked about the concept of 'I have done well'. This attitude is most apparent when people talk about property. I would now like to demolish the myth related to our peculiar relationship with property. Let's start with my favourite catch cry: 'If you want to make money out of property, don't own it'.

The table on page 95 shows the growth of earnings per share over a three- and a five-year period. It also shows dividends per share and the net tangible assets of two related businesses. On inspection, which of these two would you prefer to invest in? Bear in mind that they are both related to the Lowy family (Westfield shopping centres, where most of us will have shopped at some stage).

		3 YEARS	5 YEARS
Westfield Hldgs to 31 Dec 2002	**EPS**	16.01%	20.05%
	DPS	16.20%	20.58%
	NTA	37.43%	32.90%
Westfield Trust to 31 Dec 2002	**EPS**	2.11%	2.83%
	DPS	2.11%	2.84%
	NTA	4.53%	5.15%

Source: S&P/ASX

Earnings per share (EPS): A measure of a company's performance, calculated by dividing the company's net operating profit after tax by the number of shares on issue.

Dividends per shares (DPS): The proportion of a company's earnings paid to shareholders.

Net Tangible Assets (NTA): Total assets of a company less total liabilities, and not including intangible items like goodwill.

My guess is that your answer to my first question would be Westfield Holdings. My next question is: Which of these did the Lowy family own? The answer was Westfield Holdings. Which was the one most popular with the public? Westfield Trust of course; particularly as it enjoyed a higher yield! I will comment on this shortly.

The reason the Lowy family owned Westfield Holdings was because it didn't own property. Westfield Trust owned all of that. Westfield Holdings had the management, development and construction rights to all the physical property that the Lowy family were smart enough *not to own*.

A similar situation applied to Lend Lease and General Property Trust (GPT). GPT owns all the property. Lend Lease develops, manages, constructs and refurbishes, but *generally* doesn't own property either. If you want to make money out of property, the general rule is simple: find the trust that owns the physical property, then find the management company that sits behind it and buy that!

One of the difficulties with all of the above is that for retirees in particular, Westfield Holdings, Lend Lease and so on, offered lower yields. This made them unattractive in the income stakes for investors. This is where the yield trap bit the hardest.

Let's take an example. The table below shows two investments. In 1984 my wife invested $1,000 in Westfield Holdings. At the same time, I invested the same amount in Westfield Trust (I was after the income!). At the end of the first year, we both receive our dividend cheques. As you can see, I have clearly had the better income in Year 1.

PROPERTY – TO OWN OR NOT?

$1,000 Invested in 1984

	Westfield Holdings	Westfield Trusts
Dividend 1st Yr	$61.00	$92.00
Yield	6.1%	9.2%
Dividend 2002	$2,057.00	$168.00
Value 2002	$131,091.00	$2,500.00
Yield	1.6%	6.7%

Compiled by MLC Investments Ltd
Source: J B Were & Son Quant. Research

We now come to the present. We both still hold our original investments and we have taken dividends each year. We both received our latest dividends on the same day. As you can see, my income has risen over the period but not to the same degree as my wife's. Adding insult to injury, the value of my wife's investment has far outstripped mine. The only consolation is to point out what a pathetic yield my wife is currently receiving!

Let me make one final point on this issue. Whilst Westfield Holdings and Trust is a great example of how to make money by not owning property, let me highlight how substantial the difference is. An investment of $1,000 in Westfield Holdings, when it went public, would today be worth over $148,000,000. Remember, this period is the average working lifespan. Not bad for not owning property.

It is with some sadness that I must acknowledge the loss of this great engine of wealth creation. Westfield Holdings and the associated property trusts have now been *stapled* together as a single entity. Whilst a great story comes to an end, the principle remains true.

For all you property owners out there who feel comfortable in the knowledge that you have *done well* out of property: Let me remind you that the reason you feel that way is because your standards or benchmarks are so low. You simply compare yourself with other property owners.

CHAPTER SEVENTEEN
THE SHARE MARKET — FRIEND OR FOE?

Our perceptions play a vital role in determining how we respond to events in the world around us. Our attitudes to the share market are no exception. When you look at the press and its treatment of the market ups and downs, it is little wonder that many of us have a poor perception of the share market.

Interestingly, the volatility mentioned earlier makes the market exciting and reportable. Imagine what would happen if the prices of houses in each suburb were run across the top of the television screen each night. The volatility of the housing market would soon become as much a part of our everyday awareness as the weather or the stock market.

Our perceptions of the share market are powerfully influenced by the daily reporting of trends in newspapers and on evening news. Every share price is quoted minute by minute; however, we fail to comprehend that what we are viewing is the price, not the value. The daily values of businesses change about as much as the daily value of your house, but it's the price of the business that is quoted, not the value. Shares are auctioned every day under everybody's gaze. A single property is rarely auctioned twice in the same year!

As a consequence, our relationship with property tends to be emotional, irrational and positive. Our relationship with the share market, on the other hand, tends to be emotional, irrational and negative. If we look at some of the headlines over time it is instructive.

A $6.9bn share plunge

WORLD MELTDOWN

This is a tiny part of my collection of financial *pornography*. We never see property reported in the same way and we are also unlikely to ever see the headline: *Share Market Rise!* As a result, we perceive the share market as unpredictable and volatile. It has all the ingredients for gambling, and as a result we tend to see only the negatives.

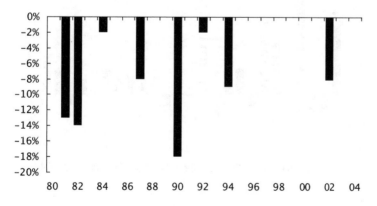

Annual Returns of Australian Shares*

Source: S&P/ASX

Year Ending 31 December

99

The graph on page 99 shows the negative years since 1979. Most of us could reel off the reasons why they were negative: the drought in Australia in 1981-1982; the share market crash of 1987; the Gulf war in 1990; the Global financial market *meltdown* in 1994, and finally, the crash in 2002.

Regrettably, it is this image that remains in most people's minds. Consider how many times the spectre of the 1987 *crash* has been raised. It seems as though every year we are reminded of that *disaster* or warned to look out for a repeat. The craziest example of this was October 1997, when the press was encouraging us to celebrate the tenth anniversary of the 1987 crash with a repeat crash. Just to jog your memories, consider the following headlines:

$1billion-a-minute freefall

THE SHARE CRASH OF '97

If we now add the positive years to the graph we see a stark contrast.

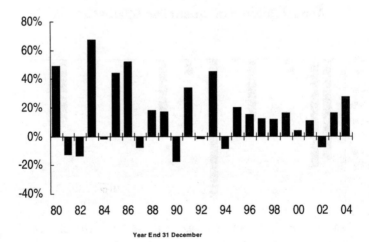

Annual Returns of Australian Shares - All Ords Index

Year End 31 December

Source: S&P/ASX

Despite the outrageous headlines, 1997 was a positive year for the market. You can see quite clearly that the positive years far outnumber the negative ones; and that the magnitude of the rises is far greater than the magnitude of the falls. You can see that despite the outrageous weather pattern, the climate is benign!

These simple facts are what drive the long-term outcome of investing in productive enterprise. Despite the short-term volatility, the future direction of the share market is upwards! This is because the share market reflects human endeavour. Industry does not exist as a mere plaything for the idle rich. It exists because it meets our needs.

Companies that make irrelevant products that no one wants don't survive for long outside a command economy (Russia and China are recent past examples). As our needs become more sophisticated, new and vibrant companies rise to meet the challenge; old companies reinvent themselves, some fail and die, but the process continues as it has for centuries with only an increase in the sophistication.

In the graph on page 99, I used an expanded scale to illustrate the falls. In the graph on page 100, those losses were presented in the perspective of the gains over other years. The first chart reflects how newspapers and commentators perceived these losses. This loss-aversion is true to life.

As I mentioned earlier in the book, academic studies have discovered that we feel our losses more than twice as acutely as we enjoy our gain. Our perception amplifies the magnitude of an event if that event is a negative one. We tend to overstate our losses, and understate our gains. This is not a good emotional background for sensible investing, but it is an aspect of our nature that we should be aware of when making decisions.

At the end of each year I will continue to add the next bar to the graph on page 100. The erratic pattern will continue; more ups than downs, and bigger rises than falls. Do you feel that futher negative bars will make any difference to the long-term wealth creation prospects of Australian shareholders in industry? I suspect your answer is the same as mine: NO! So what is it that scares many existing and also prospective shareholders? The answer, as always, is fear — and that fear is based on ignorance. We fear what we do not understand. Knowledge is power. If we approach the discipline of investing in a cavalier manner, is it any wonder things go wrong? We have no clear sense of the outcomes and are disappointed when things don't work out the way we wanted. Worst of all, many people have the gall to blame the share market for their woes. A high IQ doesn't help in these circumstances. There are probably just as many scared academics trying to invest sensibly as there are others. It is our EQ, however, that is crucial in influencing our investment endeavours.

We need to understand that the market is benign; it is truly a market where we can exchange — for value — ownership of productive enterprise. It is our friend; and provided it is treated with respect, it creates appropriate wealth for all those who use it sensibly. However, if we approach it as a gambler, we need to be prepared for the inevitable outcome.

Here is a similar graph to the previous one except it is over the last century. Notice that it shows a similar pattern.

Annual Returns of Australian Shares - All Ords Index

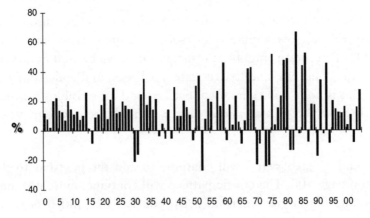

To Year End 31 December 2004

Source: S&P/ASX

As a final blow on behalf of investors, I would make the following outrageous statement: 'The future direction of the share market will be upwards!'

CHAPTER EIGHTEEN
WHAT CRASH?

We often hear people talking about past cataclysmic share market crashes, 1929 and 1987 in particular. We are reminded again and again of how long it took for the share market to recover to the high levels that existed before the crash. This is the argument many critics of the share market use. 'Downturns and crashes are inevitable,' they argue. 'That is why you need to develop a balanced portfolio (i.e. a mix of shares, cash and property). It's a strategy that will enable you to avoid those long periods where shares don't perform well.'

It is worth looking closely at what actually happens when there is a crash. Take the 1929-30 crash: The Dow Jones Index in the United States hit a peak on the 7th September, 1929. By the 29th October, a mere seven weeks later, it had dropped 40 per cent. What observers fail to mention is that the market had risen by 51 per cent in the 12 months immediately prior, and a whopping 80 per cent in the 21 months prior to the correction. The Crash of '29 appeared to be devastating; but we need to understand that it was no more than a correction of the irrational exuberance that preceded it. To take an irrational peak and then measure how long it took to get back to this irrational level is frankly, irrational!

Let's look at our market in the much-touted Crash of '87. When you look at the chart below, put your finger on the crash of 1987. Clearly, the crash did not exist. The reason is quite simple. All I have done is delete 12 months of data from the chart.

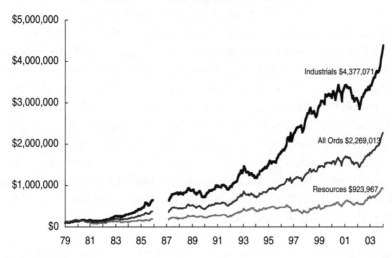

Where is the *crash* of '87?
$100,000 Invested December 1979-2004

Source: S&P/ASX

The arithmetic is as follows: if I double one I end up with two. If I halve two, I end up with one. That is the basic arithmetic; now let me relate it to the graph. From October 1986 to October 1987, the All Ordinaries Index rose by 100 per cent. From October 1987 it fell by 50 per cent and ended up exactly where it had been 12 months earlier. Shock horror! How quickly we forget that in the 12 months prior to this correction, the index had almost doubled. The irrational peak became the benchmark against which all future movements would be measured. Sure, it took the index nearly three years to get back to the previous high, but I would argue that at the time it should not have been any where near that level anyway.

John Stuart Mill (1806-1873) summed up this attitude in Principles of Political Economy, which he wrote in 1848. His words are a suitable epitaph to 1929, 1987 and all other periods of irrational exuberance: 'The inclination of the mercantile public to increase their demand for commodities by making use of all or much of their credit as a purchasing power depends on their expectation of profit. When there is a general impression that the price of a commodity is likely to rise, from an extra demand, a short crop, obstructions to importation, or any other cause, there is a disposition among dealers to increase their stocks, in order to profit by the expected rise. This disposition tends, in itself to produce the effect which it looks forward to, a rise of price: and if the rise is considerable and progressive, other speculators are attracted, who, so long as the price has not begun to fall, are willing to believe it will continue rising. These, by further purchases, produce a further advance. Thus a rise of price, for which there were originally some rational grounds, is often heightened by merely speculative purchases, until it greatly exceeds what the original grounds will justify. After a time, this begins to be perceived; the price ceases to rise, and the holders, thinking it time to realise their gains, are anxious to sell. Then the price begins to decline: the holders rush into market to avoid a still greater loss. And, few willing to buy in a falling market, the price falls much more suddenly than it rose.'

Crashes might best be summarised as follows: the prelude is all buyers and no sellers, and the finale is all sellers and no buyers. When a crash occurs, it occurs because the market has reached an unsustainable level – an irrational high. What history shows us is that after every crash, there is gradual, solid recovery.

CHAPTER NINETEEN
OKAY, OKAY!! BUT WHICH SHARES SHOULD I BUY?

By now, you may have accepted the arguments presented in these pages. However, a key question remains unanswered: 'I agree, but which shares do I buy?' Human nature seems to dictate that we try and do everything ourselves. However, we don't need to be a *Jack-of-All-Trades* and consequently, master of none.

If we set out without goals, with unrealistic expectations, without clear standards concerning what we hope to achieve, the result is likely to be mediocrity. Successful people identify what it is they are good at and, with focus, become brilliant at that one discipline. They can then afford to outsource most functions that fall outside their areas of strength — they can delegate those responsibilities to other people.

Despite the much-vaunted benefits of technology, we are even more time-poor today than previously. The stresses associated with trying to juggle careers and personal lives to achieve balance grow all the time, and are well documented. The belief that we can do everything is more and more an illusion.

Investing is no different. We need to be clear on this score: Wisdom in the field of investing, as in all fields of human endeavour, comes with experience and time. Now and then, an amateur achieves spectacular results; but it is usually a case of good luck, not good judgment.

The best advice I can offer is this: Outsource things to others to achieve the best result. We are not allowed to perform medical operations upon one another. We seek legal guidance from professionals. We use engineers to build roads, bridges and tall buildings. We can't drive or fly without a licence. Yet in the field of investing, people sometimes entrust their future wealth to amateurs and fools. We often don't care whom we obtain financial advice from, as long as we don't pay for it. Well-meaning parents may sit down with their children and advise. What expertise do they have in this area? Good intentions don't qualify. Would we ask our stockbroker to solve our medical problems?

Identify your core competency, work hard to become brilliant at that thing and outsource your limitations to competent professionals. If you do that, it changes the questions from, 'Which shares should I buy?' to 'How much can I afford to invest? Which assets do I feel most comfortable with?' If your comfort is with sub-optimal assets for the long term, your next step is to identify a mentor or teacher who will provide the extra knowledge and eventually the comfort for you to optimise your financial position.

This process will involve some changes in attitude. The most important of these will be to acknowledge, as painful as it may be for some, that the majority of us will live a great deal longer than we think. This places a greater burden on the decision-making process. Assets that we may have been comfortable with will become inappropriate, and assets that we are least comfortable with will become appropriate.

Having come this far you should have identified how much you are prepared to commit for your future and also identified the most appropriate asset class or classes for you.

It is interesting to note that the labeling of funds by some managers may not give you any clue as to what the fund is trying to achieve. Most prospectus commentary is a lot of general blather that doesn't give the investor a strong sense of how the manager intends to produce the results, particularly from the point of view of portfolio turnover. Remember that whether we speculate with our money or the fund manager speculates with it, the result may end up the same.

With some equity funds, the labeling has been particularly misleading. It has been apparent for many years that a number of the so-called imputation funds that have been available for retail investors were nothing more than trading funds despite their titles. High levels of distributed gains at the end of the year can make a mockery of any gearing strategies using these high turnover funds.

This is not meant to be a definitive chapter on 'How to choose a fund manager'; that is the role of a financial advisor. It simply seeks to identify some of the issues you must be aware of as you navigate the world of investing. For those of you more interested in the *nuts and bolts,* the centre pages of the Australian Financial Review list all industrial and resource shares under separate headings. So if you are confused about a particular stock, this is the place to go. Question your fund manager and advisor until you are comfortable that both you and they are aligned with the investment strategy.

Finally, all you need to do longer term is fine-tune your strategy with appropriate products as your circumstances change, and then *STICK TO IT!* It is this final element of discipline that can ensure a positive outcome for any of us. In doing this, don't fall into the trap of allowing perceptions of the share market to stand in the way. Property has great appeal because of its tangibility. It is difficult to conjure up a coherent image when talking about shares.

Just remember that the share market reflects human endeavor. Share markets, in one form or another, have existed for centuries. How many computer and airline companies could our grandparents invest in? How many automotive and camera companies could they invest in? How many companies were making magnetic resonance body scanners in 1930? How many companies make metal spears for warfare today?

Most of us get out of bed in the morning and eat breakfast. As a shareholder in most of Australia's food companies, I sigh gratefully. We clothe ourselves, we move around our environment. We telephone our friends and work colleagues. We demand ever more sophisticated travel, entertainment and health care.

As long as the human race continues to strive (for better or worse), there will be businesses that you and I can invest in. As the preservation of this planet takes precedence over its exploitation, new companies will appear that will enable you and I to invest in a sustainable future.

CHAPTER TWENTY
PERCEPTIONS VERSUS REALITY

Perception is reality. In the next part of this book, I deal with some of these perceptions and how they can often be barriers to successful progress — and not just in the area of personal finance.

I have presented in public forums thousands of times and as a result I enjoy a relatively privileged position; I receive feedback from people almost every day of my working life. In this chapter I am going to expose some of my *perceptions* as a result of this feedback. Many people have written books on the link between money and personality, so I will not re-run the issue. I am aware that these comments will be generalisations. I am not standing in judgment, but simply making observations — you may agree or disagree.

The word *retirement* conjures up all sorts of images in peoples' minds. The advertisements on television show happy, healthy couples, walking along a sunny beach; people cruising in a huge powerboat, or strolling the deck of an ocean liner. This is the dream! The reality is that most of us will never achieve these, apart from maybe once in a lifetime.

Let me give a definition of retirement.

The word RETIRE (and its close relatives: RETIRED, RETIREMENT, RETIREMENT VILLAGE, RETIRING) conjures up a variety of images.

To retire is to leave employment, especially because of age. To retire is to withdraw, to retreat, to go away, to seek peace and seclusion. Some people choose to live a retiring life; they seek out a quiet, out-of-the-way place where they can enjoy their seclusion. Such people are often called retiring; they are shy, preferring seclusion and separateness from others.

Retirement refers to the decision to cease work; and once I have retired, I am in retirement.

Retirement refers to that period of a person's life that follows the act of retirement. Some people even enter a Retirement Village — a complex of separate dwellings, or at the least, self-contained units in which retired people live.

The picture these words conjure up does not resemble those created by hyperactive advertising agencies. Despite our dreams, this is closer to reality for most of us than the *dream*.

Every few years the Australian Bureau of Statistics conducts a census. In the 1996 census, an interesting piece of information went unpublished, although the data was collected. The bureau looked at the incomes of all age groups; the horrifying statistic is that in the age group 65 years and over more than 80 per cent of people are on incomes of less than $15,000 per annum. So much for the ocean liner and the beachside home! Only a tiny 0.7 per cent of the population over 65 years of age enjoy incomes of $70,000 or more. These are the ones that appear in the advertisements.

A further release of bureau data bears out my observations. People aged over 65 spend, on average, 12 hours and 26 minutes of their waking day without any human contact. For some, this may be fine, but for those who need human contact, it is deadly. It is estimated that in 30 years, the over 65s will comprise over 20 per cent of the population and they will spend up to 80 per cent of their time alone.

This has implications for all of us. For most of us, interchange and emotional contact with other human beings makes our lives worth living. You could be the richest person and yet the most miserable. Money doesn't guarantee happiness or longevity. This is where our emotional intelligence is so important. It is our EQ that affects how we use what money we have and why.

As a general rule, I observe that women cope well with change, whilst men do not. Women experience a great deal of change during their lives: education, workforce, family, workforce and then retirement. For many women, retirement is just a part of the ever-changing pattern of life; and for many it allows an expansion of interests. As a counterpoint, men generally undertake little in the way of change; their life pattern is: education, workforce and retirement.

I do not consider voluntary job changing to be a change, unless it involves a huge directional shift (i.e. nuclear physicist to overseas voluntary aid worker).

The impact of this *stereotyping* is not apparent until retirement, when it arrives with a vengeance.

Studies have indicated a major risk to males in retirement. Research established that men tend to be:

• less socially competent
• less socially confident
• less inclined to make new friends
• less outgoing
• less inclined to try new ventures outside the house.

Women rely less on their jobs to define themselves. They have a better sense of identity. Men tend to define themselves by their careers. Many times at seminars, retired men will introduce themselves and will describe themselves as an ex-engineer, builder, manager, pharmacist, pilot, plumber, and so on. It is what males have done for most of their adult lives; their career helped to define their identities and their place in society. When that definition is removed at retirement, many men are left with a lack of self-worth and identity. Many have lost their dream.

Many try to fill the vacuum with a part-time job. However, once the *part-time* day job has gone, the vacuum again becomes apparent. There are 24 hours of the day to be filled; there is a life to be lived. As with personal finances, it will require careful thought and planning if it is to be satisfying and fruitful.

My main point in saying this is: *Build an income stream that will grow over time. Couple this with valuable human relationships and you have a successful retirement.* You have done well!

CHAPTER TWENTY-ONE
HOW OLD IS *TOO OLD*?

I have observed over many years another fundamental difference in the attitudes of men and women. In my parents' era, this problem barely existed; however it is now fast becoming one — there is a growing gap between my perception of time frames and that of others. This gap has now become a gulf.

Consider the following time frames for investment and then ask yourself how you feel about such time frames.

Long term = 10 years
Medium term = 5 years
Short term = 1 year

The normal response is, 'Yes, that sounds reasonable.' My response is, 'What a pity!' My definitions of investment time frames are as follows:

Long term = your lifetime and beyond
Medium term = about 30–40 years
Short term = around 10 years

Any less and you are just a *mug punter!* Does anyone disagree? Nine times out of ten I get disagreement. Usually it is the males who disagree — or occasionally a female speaking on behalf of the male sitting beside her.

The disagreement takes many forms but has the same underlying theme.

Having just retired, a couple was queried about why they had replaced their relatively new car. The male response: 'Oh, I bought the new one as I've now retired. It should last me ten years and it will probably see me out.'

The event that really sparked my awareness of this as an issue occurred at a seminar some five years ago. The audience was entirely retirees and I had given my account of time frames and asked, 'Does any one disagree?' A gentleman leapt to his feet, pointed at me accusingly and said, 'It's all right for you young blokes talking about the long term, but I'm 72. I don't even buy green bananas anymore.'

The audience thought this was a huge joke and we all fell about laughing. I waited for the laughter to subside and then said forcefully, 'If that is the way you feel, do your wife a favour and die now so that she can do something sensible with your money.'

It sounds harsh, but was appropriate at the time. In conversation later, he acknowledged that there was no basis for what he had said; it was simply one of those reflexes that males have acquired over the years. His wife was even more forthcoming. As she shook my hand she said, 'I want to thank you... you've done what I've wanted to do for 11 years — *tell him to die*. But I could never find the words.'

They clearly cared for one another, but his defeatist and careless comments were beginning to wear thin. As life spans extend, older couples are together for longer and longer. I had intuitively hit upon a key issue. In seminars, I started to push the boundaries further. When I related this incident to other audiences, I watched the body language closely. It became clear that there was considerable female support for my view, and much male discomfort. I pushed the boundaries a bit further.

At a seminar some weeks later, I suggested that the men consider the fact that they will live a great deal longer than they think, and that they should do it with dignity because the women were sick and tired of the male love affair with mortality. What a shock! The women burst into spontaneous applause. Each time I explore the limits of this issue; I find the result is the same. Women are tired of the flippant male perspective on life spans.

This, in addition to the financial aspect, is simply one other issue that must be addressed before retirement. I don't know whether I expect too much of people, but I think a deep respect for one's partner is vital to the successful ageing for us all. It is almost as if the suggestion of imminent demise removes all possible response and absolves the male of any really hard thought about the future.

For many years it was the male prerogative to handle the *finances* in the household. As a result, many financial planning decisions that I see today are male-centred. Many men do not expect an extended lifespan in retirement and choose a short-term secure *fix*. It must be understood that statistically women will outlive men, so that all decisions should be related to the woman's potential lifespan and not what the man thinks his may be.

Take your superannuation payout; buy a four-wheel drive and a caravan. Put a bumper sticker on the rear: 'We are on a SKI holiday' — (SKI stands for Spending the Kids' Inheritance.) When the superannuation is spent, settle down on the old age pension. 'Is that all there is?'

We need to remember that we will all be a long time in retirement and if we have all had an *active* working life, we shouldn't let that end at retirement. That is how we become irrelevant.

You are now the managing director or joint managing director (with your partner) of a business called *Future Life Pty Ltd*. You will need to spend a great deal of time and energy planning and running this business if it is to be successful. If not, it will go the way of all businesses that suffer neglect or poor planning and management.

As far as investment decisions are concerned, think beyond your lifespan and that of your spouse; think of your children, your children's children and eternity.

CHAPTER TWENTY-TWO
WHERE TO FROM HERE?

In most of the previous graphs I have separated income and capital to give you a clear understanding of the two-dimensional nature of assets. The *income* (which is the interest paid on a term deposit, the rent from property and the profit or dividend from a business or share), the *value* (which is the long-term price of these same assets, term deposits, property and shares) and whether you choose to acknowledge these factors in combination, is entirely your call.

In the graph on page 120, I have combined the two factors again. (For ease of explanation, assume that retirees who are judging the quality and value of retirement income can use the previous graphs where I have separated income and capital.)

This graph is for people who are still working and not of a mind to distinguish between income and growth. They only look at the total result as their superannuation account balance grows year after year.

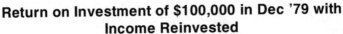

Return on Investment of $100,000 in Dec '79 with Income Reinvested

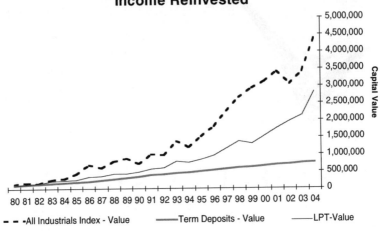

- - -All Industrials Index - Value   ——Term Deposits - Value   ——LPT-Value

Source: S&P/ASX

It is apparent that the *pecking* order of the assets remains intact over the longer term. A term deposit with all the interest reinvested would have accumulated $760,000. Property and shares would have accumulated $2.8 and $4.3 million respectively. The differences are obvious.

As a final blow in my effort to push the reluctant amongst you over the line, consider the following: I have had the following issue raised many times in public seminars; it may be summarised as follows:

'It is all well and good, what you have said, but the share market is at an all time high (or falling) and I feel very nervous about investing at the moment.'

The market *is* always at an all time high or falling, and I understand your nervousness. This is because you are reading the graph right to left. If, like me, you are interested in the future, then you will read left to right. From where I stand today, in the year 2005, the share market is at an all time low compared to the future (which is to the right NOT the left). What it will do in the short term — in five to ten years — is pretty irrelevant to me. That smacks of weather forecasting!

There are three kinds of people in the world:

• those who make things happen
• those who watch it happen
• and those who are heard to exclaim, 'Jeez, what happened'?

In the spirit of the former, I offer the following comment. Many people seem completely paralysed by the past, and incapable of creating their futures. By now, people in this category will have stopped reading this book. When they attend my seminars, I urge them to go home and at least encourage their own children to look forward.

As a public speaker I suffer from a major shortcoming. I cannot tell jokes to save my life. I enjoy what is referred to as the *lowest form of wit*, which amongst perfect strangers can be off-putting to say the least. I acknowledge that in my public presentations I will probably upset a percentage of the audience. The criticism usually concerns my style, not the content. Initially, this used to upset me, as I was uncomfortable with criticism. Now, I am delighted with it. It tells me that I have captured the imaginations of the other 95 per cent of the audience. If I have not upset someone, I haven't done my job.

CHAPTER TWENTY-THREE
PHILANTHROPY

In trying to encourage people to think beyond the *normal* time frame, I am reminded of a story that appeared in the Washington Post some years ago. Although the story was about extraordinary wealth, the article was actually about philanthropy — a thing that is not well acknowledged in Australia and which I think is a reflection of our immaturity as a nation.

In the United Kingdom and the United States, most of the major educational institutions are funded by huge endowments left to them over the years by wealthy philanthropists. Such bequests are made in gratitude to these institutions for offering the skills that have allowed many to do extraordinary things in life.

In Australia, we still have a lingering suspicion of intelligence as it somehow smacks of elitism. As a consequence, most of our educational institutions go begging for money to the government of the day. Despite our claims of being a *clever country*, we are slow to commit either the capital or the spirit to this ideology. We expect the government to provide education and other services. We expect to pay as little as possible, and with our busy lives, do not give of our selves.

Donald Othmer and his wife, Mildred, lived quiet and unpretentious lives. Donald was a professor of chemical engineering in Brooklyn, who contributed to more than 40 patents at Eastman Kodak. Donald died in 1995. His wife, a former teacher and a buyer for her mother's dress store, died in 1998. They were described as 'living comfortably but not ostentatiously, and rarely ever talked about their money.'

This was why it came as a shock to their friends to learn that their combined estates were worth $800 million, and that they had given nearly everything to charity. The obvious question was: 'How did they become so rich?' Their formula was simple; they put their money into sound stock market investments and left it there.

When I relate this story, people often respond with: 'How foolish! Why didn't they spend it — they couldn't take it with them.' Many people hold the attitude: 'I want to spend my last dollar on the day I die.'

The Othmers' estate will provide $190 million to Brooklyn Polytechnic University where Donald taught, $160 million to Long Island College Hospital, $75 million to Planned Parenthood and so on.

Having worked at Perpetual Trustees in Sydney for a number of years, I became interested in some of the charitable trusts that were established by Australian philanthropists. The Archibald prize for art (now administered by the NSW government), the Paul Lowin Music Award and the Ramaciotti Foundation for Medicine are just a few.

Clive and Vera were the children of Major General Gustavo Ramaciotti. He arrived from Italy with his family when he was only a child in the middle of the 1800s, and practised in Sydney as a lawyer.

Major General Ramaciotti, who achieved this rank during World War I, bought the Theatre Royal in King Street, Sydney (now part of the MLC

Centre) in around 1913. He left it to his children, Vera and Clive — neither of whom married. Clive died in 1967, Vera 15 years later.

In 1970, Vera sold the Theatre Royal and the adjacent properties, which would prove to be to the community's lasting gain. With the proceeds, Vera established the Clive and Vera Ramaciotti Foundations, the purpose of which was to give substantial support to biomedical research — an interest shared by both Vera and her brother. The decision was also thought to have been influenced by the long family link with the Hall family and their philanthropic attitude (resulting in the Walter and Eliza Hall Institute), and also Vera's struggle with diabetes.

Both of the Clive and Vera Ramaciotti Foundations now support biomedical research. One foundation supports research in NSW, and the other supports research in the other states and territories of Australia.

The combined capital of the foundations in 2003 was over $50 million, which is managed by Perpetual Trustees. A Scientific Advisory Committee advises Perpetual on the grants to be made each year. The first grants were made in 1971, when an accumulated amount of $600,000 was distributed to 27 institutions. In 2003, the value of the more than 100 grants being made, was approximately $2 million — making the joint foundations a major private contributor to medical research in Australia.

In total, the foundations had contributed over $38 million to biomedical research across more than 3,100 research projects. Many projects, including those in areas such as molecular biology, genetics and immunology, have benefited from both laboratory and clinical support provided by the foundations.

The reason for the growth in grants from $600,000 to approximately $2 million is prudent investment in the share market and, above all else, Australian industrial shares. Imagine if these foundations had invested in *safe* term deposits!

In comparison, we could argue that the Othmer's went too far. Perhaps they should have spent $200 million during their lifetimes and bequeathed the balance. I suspect that as they died in their nineties, it just would not have felt right for them. We need to bear in mind that they were born at the turn of the last century, and they would have acquired very different values to ours.

This is where emotional intelligence has a role to play. Money created for the sake of making money is pointless. There has to be either an altruistic reason or a personal goal associated with wealth creation.

For the Othmers, there was clearly an altruistic goal. We all have the potential to create substantial wealth through patience and thrift, but it is important that we know how much is enough. Many of us have a desire to possess wealth, but often the wealth possesses us. I was reminded at a recent seminar, that I was not a *nice* person because all I talked about was money, and that I must remember, 'money is the root of all evil'. Money is not the root of all evil — *desire of money* is the root of all evil.

It is not just medicine that can benefit from philanthropy. Paul Lowin was born on 22 September 1893 in Jagerdorf in Czechoslovakia, and settled in Austria during the 1930s. Along with many others caught up in the Anschluss of 1938 he fled Vienna, arriving in Australia via Egypt in 1939.

In 1948 Paul became a naturalised Australian citizen and for 20 years carried on his business — Swedish Hand Weaving Co, a Sydney-based wholesale dealership of cloth and dry goods. From 1951 until February 1956, he worked an in absentia partnership with Ali August Landauer and Maurice Michael Watson, having returned to Vienna in the early 50s to pursue an active career as a foreign correspondent.

Paul Lowin's great passion in life was music and he regularly attended Sydney Symphony Orchestra Concerts.

Mrs L Krips, widow of Henry Krips who lived near Paul in Sydney in 1939, wrote that, 'Paul Lowin came to our place very often, badly in need of communicating about music. He took singing lessons at the time and Lieder was his great love. Paul Lowin was a rather lonely person full of ideas and cultural ambitions, rather colourful.'

Karl Bittman, co-author of *Strauss to Matilda* — a book dedicated to the contribution of Austrians to Australian culture — remembers Paul Lowin singing in one of the many concerts Viennese refugees staged in their early days in Sydney.

Ali Landauerer, in a letter recalling his association with Paul remembers, 'Mr. Lowin used to sing at private parties. He had an excellent musical memory and could hum many passages from operas and operettas.'

Paul Lowin died in Vienna in 1961, leaving a Will that indicated his wish to establish a competition for works by living Australian composers in a *modern, but not too modern,* style. Due to the lack of clarity in the Will, there ensued a 30 year sustained effort by the executors of his estate to establish a viable composer competition.

The successful creation of a trust deed for the Paul Lowin Awards, ultimately approved by the Chief Justice of New South Wales, was the work of leading Sydney solicitor and musical activist, Kenneth W Tribe, AC. He has facilitated countless musical causes over the last 40 years and is the Patron of the Paul Lowin Awards.

Today the awards stand as the richest prizes for music composition in Australia.

There is an oft quoted verse in the Bible where Jesus asks what was a key question then, and what remains a key question now: 'What does it profit a person to gain the world, but to lose his soul?' The question goes to the heart of the matter: On what set of values do we base our lives? What is our purpose in accumulating wealth? What are the things that really matter to us?

Each of the *case studies* in this chapter tells the story of people who accumulated wealth, but who were driven not by the desire to be rich for the sake of it, but by the desire to use their wealth to make a difference. They are stories of passionate people, people who saw life as a *daring adventure.*

I believe that the basic principles of achieving wealth are clear and simple:

1. Be clear about time frames. Don't become extravagantly enthusiastic during those times when the market is running high; but equally, don't be despondent during the downturns. Take the long-term view.

2. Make a clear distinction between your ASSETS and your LIABILITIES. Assets are those uses of your money that bring in more money; liabilities are those things that cost you. Use your assets to create income.

3. Of the various forms of investment — property, term deposits and shares — it is the latter which yield the most consistently positive results. Yes there are some risks, but these risks can be minimised through diversifying your investments. What I have sought to demonstrate in this book is that it is investment in shares that will yield the best long-term results, creating an income stream that will sustain you throughout your retirement. And that is no mean feat!

CHAPTER TWENTY-FOUR
PUTTING THE THEORY INTO PRACTICE —
A REAL LIFE STORY

I am indebted to one man for the inspiration he gave me to write this book. Let's call him Roger.

I first met him in 1991 when he wrote to me after attending a presentation. What he doesn't know is that he became my mentor and role model.

Until I met Roger, I had worked both in Australia and overseas for a number of financial institutions in middle management roles. Nothing to shoot the lights out, but life had been fun and relatively stress free. I had learnt a great deal along the way. Whenever I stopped learning, I moved. I was always involved in dealing with people and their finances, and had come to recognise that there is a huge amount of emotional baggage that people bring to the financial decision-making process.

Roger's influence on me has been by osmosis; there was no sudden awakening. Two things appealed to me about Roger: his practical commonsense approach and his *joie de vivre*. Here he was, in his 80s, and more alive than many 30 year olds. He has immense emotional intelligence. He rules his wealth, and not the other way around. I never met the Othmers, but I know Roger well and in an Australian context, I consider that he has *done well*. I will let him tell his story!

I was brought up by my mother in the depression years. For my mother, they were hard times. I remember going to school barefoot and eating bread and dripping. We lived in just one room till I was 16, in a semi-detached house, which she rented when it became available. I remember, we let one of the other rooms for one pound a week.

At Mosman school I went bare-footed with a lot of other children, as money was scarce in the early 30s. As a child growing up in Balmoral, I played a lot of sport and was good at it; and in all I had a good time — that was where I learnt to be a good swimmer. I collected bottles off the beach and sold newspapers for pocket money — old newspapers not new ones. My mother worked for my uncle in Sydney. The fact that we had no money made me want to get it when I was in a position to do so — that made me keener as I grew up with nothing.

I left school at 16, and after being unemployed was lucky to obtain a position in the investment ledgers at Perpetual Trustees in 1938. I had never heard of shares. In those days we sat on 5-foot high stools and posted all movements in clients' assets in ledgers along a 20-foot desk. The ledgers were as big as motorcar wheels and the girls couldn't lift them.

This went on for years, and in the meantime, I wrote up the huge ledgers by hand on what the clients bought and sold, what dividends they paid and where share prices went over the long term. This entailed knowing a lot about companies listed on the exchange, and what and when their dividends were paid. I became interested in how money was invested and how it soon increased in value.

The office was hard; we worked back three or four nights each month balancing the ledgers. When we left to go to the war we jumped for joy. The depression was still severe and the management was hard on staff. To us it was an adventure.

I married an 18-year-old girl from Newcastle in 1946 prior to my discharge and returned to the office. She had no money either and we lived with my mother in a rented semi-detached cottage for seven years until we had enough for deposit on a house in Mosman. Looking back I guess the urge to make money was triggered by my mother struggling all her life for me. Here I was among hundreds of company clients working out how much they were worth. The penny had to drop!

At 55 I attended a touch-typing school and learned to type. This was necessary, as I wrote and had a book published on how to train a dog. We didn't have any children, though we tried, we had dogs instead and I became an obedience judge with the Canine Council. Since then we have travelled all over the world judging and giving lectures on how dogs are trained. My wife also worked at a haberdashery shop for about 20 years and then went to work at Franklins.

I left the office in 1980 when I retired with about $300,000, and as you can see I have benefited. I rarely sell; just purchase more when they drop. I didn't have a big portfolio initially, only about six holdings. When I retired my knowledge of equities and how the exchange worked was extensive, and I am of the opinion that with time the future of the general share market will out-perform all other types of investment.

From my experience in the company, I knew good equities grew and appreciated in value. In that regard my love of equities won the day. There was one other popular avenue that I resisted — that was to accept high interest rates that were available. I chose instead to accept poor returns from shares.

Despite my view, some folk are sensitive when it comes to buying shares and worry whenever the price slips back — I don't recommend shares for them. Share people have to grasp the nettle and buy more when there is a slump — and learn to go to sleep with a smile on their face.

At 83, I still work as a columnist. All my time is taken up training dogs. My wife is also involved. As a senior judge with the NSW Canine Council, I judge and compete all over Australia. I am a chief instructor and give regular lectures and demonstrations with my dogs.

One thing is true — when a person retires it is the most important part of their life. It is not like losing a leg when you retire — there is more in everyone than spending eight hours a day in the office.'

None of this does justice to the powerful simplicity of the man. From humble beginnings he has created a tribute to thrift and patience. He and his wife Enid cannot spend the income that they now generate. To give some sense to the story, let me now finish it.

I have met Roger on many occasions and watched his portfolio grow in value: $2 million, $3 million and most recently over $6 million. None of this is of anything other than academic interest to Roger and me.

When Roger retired his income at Perpetual was about $13,500 a year. His investment portfolio in his first year of retirement yielded about 5.5 per cent or $11,000. He retired on two-thirds of his final salary. When I met Roger in 1991, his portfolio had grown to approximately $1.3 million. Not one of his investments had gone bust in 1987, as they were too boring to be noticed by anyone.

The essence of this story is seeing that the income stream his portfolio now produces is currently just under $300,000 p.a. and growing (a yield of approximately 4 per cent).

To give a slightly bizarre slant to this, let me quote him: *'I have a policy to try and buy 10,000 shares. I look upon that as a nice neat* *number. I must stress, and it takes time to do this, have at least $100,000 in your bank account at all times. You need to be ready to buy when...'* Read those words again slowly.

This man has earned more income since he retired than he did in 42 years of work! He is no superman; he is no more intelligent than you or I. He has a high level of emotional intelligence and was able to harness some valuable knowledge. Any one of us can do the same. One of my simple goals in life, and there aren't many, is to do what Roger has done, but to do it before I retire not when I am retired.

I am not going to finish this book with the obligatory 'my wife now drives a Porsche, I have a Rolls Royce and a Ferrari and we live in a multi-million dollar home.' If that is what motivates you, then this book is a waste of time. I live in a modest house; the latest model car we drive remains a 1991 Volvo, (no jokes please); however, we can do what we wish when we wish — rent cars, houses, boats and planes. We don't need to own any of them to feel good about ourselves.

The greatest asset we have and cherish is our connection with other people and our ability to spend time with them. The winter of our lives will be filled with rich colour, images and shared words. This is the dream we live.

What's yours?

Orderform

Order the Motivated Money book by mailing or faxing your credit card details or
alternatively by mailing us a cheque.

Price: $30.00 incl GST
Postage and handling for orders within Australia: $3.70
For multiple copies to the same address, the postage and handling remains $3.70 as
I will absorb any additional postage costs.
For international orders please contact us.
Fax your completed order to us on: 02 9498 5233
or mail it to:
Motivated Money Pty Ltd
P.O. Box 527
Gordon NSW 2072

PLEASE PRINT CLEARLY

Your email address

Your first name

Your family name

Your phone number (Please include your area code)

Number of books

YOUR CREDIT CARD DETAILS

Your credit card type ☐ Visa ☐ Mastercard ☐ BankCard

Your card number ☐☐☐☐ ☐☐☐☐ ☐☐☐☐ ☐☐☐☐

Full name on card (This is the full name of the card holder NOT the bank name.)

Expiry month ☐☐ Expiry year ☐☐

DELIVERY ADDRESS

Name or Company name

ABN

Address

City or suburb

State   Postcode